Jesus is the Answer

I just wanted you to know

By Derek McCracken

www.xulonpress.com

Table of Contents

The faith question 11
Peace that passes understanding 19
Real confidence 25
Leading a disciplined life..29
The power of prayer..33
Our walk talks 42
Healthy relationships 47
The right direction..53
Seven days a week 58
When trials come 62
The gift of encouragement 70
The room under the stairs 74
The power of sowing and reaping..78
When we fail 85
satan with a small s 90
Jesus the leader 96
The power of the father..100
There is a place for you..104
The favour of God..109
Watch your tongue 114
From here 118

Introduction

The world is a truly amazing place. It's full of challenge, diversity, trial, wealth, poverty and achievement. Technologically, it is changing at an incredible rate. Yet this same world is increasingly in need of hope, with growing numbers of people looking in all the wrong places, trying to find that elusive missing ingredient called fulfilment. Without fulfilment and clear purpose, life is an existence which eventually gives way to anxiety, worry, disillusion-ment and illness. There are many questions in this life, but answers are harder to get, answers that satisfy that is.

This book is called 'Jesus is the answer, I just wanted you to know' because I've found through life experience that no one truly satisfies, no one else offers fulfilment, no one gives a life full of true purpose, other than the man Christ Jesus. All He asks is that we trust Him.

Therefore, I have written this book for those who may be considering matters of faith and to encourage those who have trusted this man called Jesus. Through the following pages it is my hope that you will be inspired to follow, grow and become more like the greatest leader and example that ever graced this earth.

A strong trusting relationship with Jesus Christ the Son of the living God is where real fulfilment is found, nowhere else.

Dedication

This book is dedicated to my family, whom I thank God for every day and love dearly.

Chapter 1

The Faith Question

A s I write this book the world is experiencing uncertainty like never before. Having said that, we probably
hold this view largely because of what we hear and see via
the media. I came across this quote recently:

> It is a gloomy moment in the history of our country. Not in
> the lifetime of most men has there been so much grave and
> deep apprehension. Never has the future seemed so uncertain.
> The domestic economic situation is in chaos. Our currency
> is weak throughout the world. The political cauldron seethes
> and bubbles with uncertainty. It is a solemn moment. Of our
> troubles no man can see the end. (Harper's Weekly Gazette,
> October 1857)

Clearly, things were uncertain back then also. The whole
global warming debate is also very topical today. A while ago
I remember hearing someone say, "according to the television news this is the warmest day we've had in 90 years." A
lady who was listening to the conversation replied, "Sure, all
that means is it was as warm as this 90 years ago, so what's
all the fuss about?" I am not saying that these issues aren't

important; all I'm saying is uncertainty has been around a long time.

A really interesting point, however, is the increase in spiritual activity. It seems like there is more talk about spiritual matters today than ever. Even television now regularly broadcasts programmes about paranormal and the supernatural. Film stars and other well known people are openly declaring their interest in religions of differing kinds. The question is why? What is causing this kind of behaviour to increase? Why the search for some spiritual experience?

The easiest way to make sense of this is to step back and look at who we are. All human beings are made the same way. We are a spirit, we have a soul, (which is made up of our mind, will and emotions) and we live in a body; that's the way we have been designed.

For example, if you have ever been around a dead person you will quickly realise that the spirit has gone; it is no longer with the body. Our spirits, therefore, are the invisible part of our make up and are often naturally described as the heart of a person; not the physical heart, but metaphorically speaking. The spirit is designed to worship and it will always be that way. If we study and research people everywhere we will see that this is true, that's why many forms of worship exist across the world today. In some of the most remote parts of the world it is amazing what people worship, but they do. Animism, for example, is a religious or spiritual idea that souls or spirits exist not only in humans, but in animals, plants and rocks. Even natural phenomena such as thunder, mountains or rivers are deemed to have spiritual power. One thing is certain: the people have an inbuilt spiritual sense or awareness, but they don't necessarily see it as spiritual. Many have a clear understanding of good and evil, with rituals forming a major part of their culture to please whatever they worship. Although difficult to explain, there is a part in every person that is the capacity to worship. It can and will be expressed in many different forms, but it is there.

I personally hold the view that there is a void inside a person spiritually until the day they meet Jesus Christ.

Why then do I say Jesus is the answer and not some other religious figure? Well the answer is really quite simple – he's alive. If you are reading this and are not a believer – don't put the book down. Take this challenge according to the book of Hebrews:

> But without faith it is impossible to please and be satisfactory to him. For whoever would come near to God must (necessarily) believe that God exists and that he is the rewarder of those who earnestly and diligently seek him (out)
>
> Hebrews 11 Verse 6 (The Amplified Bible)

If you call on the name of Jesus Christ, the son of the true God from your heart and mean it, he will answer you. Now, there is a vast difference between calling to God from your heart and calling from your head. Nobody can force or manipulate you into the kingdom of God; it's a matter between you and him. Yes, others can point out the way, but the decision is yours and only yours. When you genuinely call or cry out to him from the heart, he will respond to you. The price that was paid for you is great, so precious are you in his sight. Remember none of us can earn our way into the kingdom; all of us are to come just as we are.

It's important to realise the God referred to here is the sovereign God of Israel. Not to be confused by those who hold the view that all roads lead to God, implying that there is one God but many different ways (religions) to get to him. Not true, there is only one God that had a son called Jesus and that is Christian difference.

Those reading who are already Christians, and by this I mean, followers of Jesus, will remember clearly when you did this very thing. I personally can verify this in my own life, in my case however, I can't explain it easily, but it was clearly a supernatural event, in other words not something that I could figure out. That's the problem we have sometimes when it comes to matters of faith, if we can't work it out logically we think it can't be done. Thank God his ways are above our ways. When I flip into this mode I begin to think about a God who can count the grains of sand on a beach and who designed DNA , then I quickly submit and get back to trusting the creator of the universe instead, it's really much easier.

Those who know your name will trust in you, for you, Lord, have never forsaken those who seek you

Psalm 9 Verse 10 (The New International Version)

The power of Love

The Christian gospel is like no other. The God of heaven makes a way for us to have forgiveness and eternal life by sacrificing his son Jesus, allowing him to die a horrible death on a cross and to overcome death and the grave so that we can live forever. Jesus is alive today and is seeking to be part of our lives every minute of every day when we invite him. The cross used for his crucifixion has become a very popular symbol, with many folks wearing it as a necklace or ear rings, but in reality the cross represents a truly painful and horrendous death, let's not forget that. We don't see many ear rings symbolising the electric chair these days.

For God so greatly loved and dearly prized the world that he (even) gave up his only begotten (unique) Son, so that whoever believes in (trusts in, clings to, relies on) him shall not perish (come to destruction, be lost) but have eternal (everlasting) life.

John 3 Verse 16 (The Amplified Bible)

There are many who try to question this sacrifice and challenge the authenticity of this unique message of hope. History is full of such people who after spending much of their lifetime trying to discredit the power of the gospel, finally become believers themselves. Many well known scientists are in this group, working logically until they can no longer line up their theories with the marvel of creation. The following article summarises much of this:

The Long Silence

At the end of time, billions of people were seated on a great plain before God's throne. Most shrank back from the brilliant light before them. But some groups near the front talked heatedly, not cringing with cringing shame - but with belligerence.

"Can God judge us? How can He know about suffering?" snapped a pert young brunette. She ripped open a sleeve to reveal a tattooed number from a Nazi concentration camp. "We endured terror . . . beatings . . . torture . . . death!"

In another group a Negro boy lowered his collar. "What about this?" he demanded, showing an ugly rope burn. "Lynched, for no crime but being black!"

In another crowd there was a pregnant schoolgirl with sullen eyes: "Why should I suffer?" she murmured. "It wasn't my fault." Far out across the plain were hundreds of such groups. Each had a complaint against God for the evil and suffering He had permitted in His world.

How fortunate God was to live in Heaven, where all was sweetness and light, where there was no weeping or fear, no hunger or hatred. What did God know of all that man had been forced to endure in this world? For God leads a pretty sheltered life, they said.

So each of these groups sent forth their leader, chosen because he had suffered the most, a Jew, a negro, a person from Hiroshima, a horribly deformed arthritic, and a thalidomide child. In the centre of the vast plain, they consulted with each other. At last they were ready to present their case. It was rather clever.

Before God could be qualified to be their judge, He must endure what they had endured. Their decision was that God should be sentenced to live on earth as a man.

Let him be born a Jew. Let the legitimacy of his birth be doubted. Give him a work so difficult that even his family will think him out of his mind.

Let him be betrayed by his closest friends. Let him face false charges, be tried by a prejudiced jury and convicted by a cowardly judge. Let him be tortured.

At the last, let him see what it means to be terribly alone. Then let him die so there can be no doubt he died. Let there be a great host of witnesses to verify it.

As each leader announced his portion of the sentence, loud murmurs of approval went up from the throng of people assembled. When the last had finished pronouncing sentence, there was a long silence. No one uttered a word. No one moved.

For suddenly, all knew that God had already served His sentence.

Author Anonymous

The power of this gospel and the message of hope it offers through the power of the Holy Spirit is truly life changing.

> But the fruit of the (Holy) Spirit (the work which his presence within accomplishes) is love, joy, (gladness) peace, patience (an even temper, forbearance), kindness, goodness (benevolence), faithfulness, gentleness (meekness, humility), self-control, (self-restraint, continence). Against such things there is no law (that can bring a change)

Galatians 5: 22&23 (The Amplified Bible)

There is power in the name of Jesus

Isn't it interesting these days when you're around people who curse and swear almost without even realising they're doing it. Often they use the name of Jesus in vain. Have you ever thought about this? You never hear people going around saying 'Oh, devil' it's usually the name of the Jesus you hear.

I heard of a family in South East Asia where the mother was dying from an illness and the local religious leaders were called to come and pray with the woman. One said, 'better luck next life' the other 'sorry, there is nothing I can do for you'. The family were desperate and sought out a new missionary pastor who had just arrived to plant a church. He came and said "silver and gold I don't have, but in the name of Jesus Christ, the son of God get up and walk" he gave the family some money and told them to go and get her some food. The next week the whole family walked into his new church with the mother completely healed of her illness.

We can never take for granted the power that is in the name of Jesus and the price He paid to set us free from the law of sin and death, but we must trust Jesus for ourselves and when we do this and ask Him to come into our lives, He will change us forever. Why don't you ask Jesus to come into your life and trust Him for yourself, if you haven't already so.

All you have to do is ask and if you believe you are being challenged then I would encourage you to consider this simple prayer today.

Lord God, I acknowledge you as the one and only true God and I ask you to come into my life and change me today. I thank you for sending your son Jesus and for paying the price for my sin. I ask you to forgive my sins and my past and make me new today through the power of your Holy Spirit. I willingly give over my life completely to you and ask you to lead me into your purpose in Jesus's mighty name. Give me strength Lord in the days to come and I place my life into your care from this day forward.

Amen

If you have prayed this prayer I would encourage you to do three things

Get hold of a good Bible which you find easy to read and begin by studying the gospels of the New Testament.

Find a good Christian, Bible believing church. You will usually know it by the love the people have for you and each other

Tell three people close to you about your decision to follow Jesus.

Chapter 2

Peace that passes understanding

H ave you ever wondered what real peace looks like? All around today we seem to be surrounded by despair, fear and anxiety. The medics are prescribing more and more medication to deal with illnesses that have their root in anxiety of some kind or another. You don't need to be around someone for very long before you will know how they are, because it will usually come out of their mouth. The Bible says that out of the abundance of the heart, the mouth speaks. That really is a true saying. Sometimes it can be amazing how much despair, fear and anxiety can come out of the mouth when pressure is applied.

Yet this is something the believer should not be troubled with. If we truly understand our position as a Christian we should be in a place of peace even in the midst of natural circumstances, which are in turmoil.

I say 'should' rather than 'are' as this is an area most Christians could call 'work in progress.' We should be close enough to the word of God to know that we are not moved by what we see, or feel, but rather by what we believe.

'You don't understand' some may say, well that's why Godly peace is so powerful, it passes understanding.

The interesting thing about true Christian living is it's like swimming upstream all the time. We need to develop a lifestyle where we trust God all of the time and not just at crisis time. We have a tendency to concentrate on circumstances and problems rather than the solutions. Remember your circumstances are really only the circle in which you stand. It's as if you can't step outside the circle. Well I have good news for you; 'you can in the name of Jesus.'

I heard a statement recently:

Doubt – despairs, complains and is sad

Faith – rejoices, gives thanks and is glad

You may be reading this today and your life is not peaceful, or you're not in the place of rest. It may be for a number of reasons such as financial, health, family or work. The circumstances simply seem so big that you can't possibly see a way through them. Well, it's time to exercise your faith. Oh, and by the way, you'll generally know the time when you need to exercise your faith as it will be when you least 'feel' like it. There are a few things you can do to help.

Make sure you're in the place where you are living right, according to the principles and teaching of Christ and you are beginning to line yourself up for Godly intervention. Carry out a quick health check by asking yourself some questions such as:

Am I harbouring unforgiveness in my life? Is there someone or something I need to forgive?

Is there something I'm doing that I need to repent of, stop doing and ask God's forgiveness? Remember true repentance is to stop and turn around and go in the opposite direction.

Am I spending time with the Lord in prayer and studying his word? Am I lining up my words with God's Word? We can take for granted the fact that we have the written word of God in the Bible – something that not all believers have access to.

There are many homes where the Bible is not present, because it has not yet been made widely available, some believers are actually living with a few loose pages, or no pages at all.

Am I learning the importance of praise and worship and am I taking some time in my schedule for this? And by the way, this doesn't need to tick any boxes, but rather whatever works for you.

The above actions will place you in the position to receive from God the Father.

Thanksgiving

The Bible says:

But thanks be to God. Who gives us the victory (making us conquerors) through our Lord Jesus Christ.

1 Corinthians, chapter 15 and verse 57
(The Amplified Bible)

Whenever the problems and worries of life become so big we are not naturally inclined to thank God – but according to scripture we should. If we begin to give glory to our God regardless of circumstances we are exercising faith. If we reverse our thinking away from scenario planning around the situation and simply present everything to God and leave it there, we will begin a change process.

Rather than building a stockpile of thoughts so high that will allow worry to take over, why not give thanks to God for the simple things of life that we take so much for granted instead. I should point out that this is a 'super' natural principle in that it is beyond the natural. It's simply not natural to give thanks in the midst of a trial, and yet this is what our God wants us to do.

Both the mind and imagination are powerful and everything begins with a thought, just a thought. We begin to give place to one thought, then another thought, and before long the mind is racing along, building up a picture so real that we can almost believe it.

The bottom line is, whatever we give place to, that is, whatever we allow to dominate our thought life, we will give place to. I often wonder what it would be like if it were possible to have a computer printout of our thoughts for, say a 12 hour period, and we categorised them, what would we be giving place to in our minds?

That's a sobering thought, isn't it? If we give place to the problem, the mountain, the crisis in our lives, rather than giving place to the one who can provide the solution, we are in danger of permitting fear and anxiety to take up residence in our lives.

When we begin to thank God as a lifestyle we automatically give Him place in our lives.

I met a lady once just before Christmas, and trying to start a conversation said to her "Well, are you getting ready for the Christmas break?" As I looked at her waiting for her answer I realised even before she spoke that something was wrong.

She replied "I lost my husband and my mother 17 years ago, my only son was killed in a car accident a few years ago and my grandson died last year."

I must say this reply left me speechless – what could I say that would bring some comfort?

After trying to at least understand how she must be feeling I came away realising one thing. I have so much to thank God for. The grace of God, his unmerited favour, undeserved in my life, is something I will never take for granted. Whenever we thank God for His grace on our lives remember 'grace is not getting what we do deserve' and 'getting what we don't deserve' this keeps things in perspective.

> Casting the whole of your care (all your anxieties, all of your worries, all your concerns, once and for all) on Him, for He cares for you affectionately and cares about you watchfully

1 Peter chapter 5 and verse 7 (The Amplified Bible)

This is a passage of scripture that is one of the most challenging in the word of God. It takes faith to trust God in circumstances which are very real and tangible around us, yet this is the way we are instructed to live as Christians. We often have a tendency to trust the Lord, hand the care or situation over to Him in prayer and in a short time; we decide to take it back again. Why is this? It can be that we are not patient enough, or we have in our mind a way that it should go, or we allow it to become heavier in our thoughts and imaginations, forcing ourselves to pick it up again.

Our minds are amazing things. We can work up tremendous imagination sometimes. I know what this is like in my own life.

I have had to train myself not to race off and draw up some kind of plan in my mind for this thing and that situation – my wife will confirm this quite easily as there have been periods in my life when I have really frustrated her by being indecisive.

On reflection, I discovered that in times of change, transition or even in periods of extreme busyness, my mind would race off in all directions. Unaware of how this sounded to those close to me, I eventually realised that it caused me to resemble the man in the book of James, chapter 1 v 8 - the double minded man unstable in all his ways.

Thank God, I found the answer to this. I had to step back and organise my life in every area including work, ministry and my leisure time. I had to consider what was important, how it lined up with what I'm good at and most important what God had for me to do. As I carried out this exercise I realised that I had so many things going on in my business, my church, and spare time. I discovered that I was having difficulty in separating out passion, duty, desire and necessity to the point I was confused.

After I reviewed all areas and compartmentalised them, I was able to settle my thinking to become single-minded again and praise God the peace returned.

Chapter 3

Real confidence

Are you a confident person? Or are you like most people in the world today who have been conditioned by someone or something. What do I mean? Do you have a poor self image or a low self esteem or self worth?

I remember hearing a story of a boy who ran home from school excited to tell his father that he came second in the whole of the county in a music exam. His father said 'Son, don't you ever come first in anything?'

The boy who grew to become a man said "I am now 55 years old, I run a business where 600 people report to me every day, and I am still trying to prove myself to my own father."

The scars of this type of thing are deep and you can easily believe the lie that you are worth little and won't achieve anything of significance. That view has its root from the pit of hell but is usually delivered to you by people, often people who are close to you, family and so called friends. You will hear many opinions in this life, but remember, 'Opinions are like armpits, everybody has them, but some of them stink!'

I see many people today, young and old outwork this conditioning in different ways. Some are under achievers, procrastinators, always promising much but usually delivering less.

Others are quite obsessive at times, relentlessly trying to prove 'they can' in some capacity. The reality is that much of this behaviour is a result of some kind of rejection and a poor self image.

Consider these statements:

There is the person you think you are
There is the person others think you are
There is the person you think others think you are
There is the person you really are

Of course, as a believer, the person you really are, should be based on what God says you are, after all, the Bible says we are made in God's image. Now that takes a little working out.

We need to grasp the concept of a Godly self-image, which involves how we view ourselves, for example, 'what kind of words would you use if you were asked to describe yourself?' This is worth doing sometime, just take a few minutes and write down a brief description of yourself. Then begin to study what God says about you and ask him to reveal this to you through the power of the Holy Spirit. Here are a few verses to get you started:

Genesis 1:26-27, Genesis 9:6, Psalm 8:4-5, Ecclesiastes 7:29, Isaiah 43:7, James 3:9, Ephesians 5:1, 1 Corinthians 11:7, Colossians 3:10, 1 Peter 1:16.

If we get our Godly self-image right, when can then consider self-esteem and put a very different value on ourselves, as we will see ourselves as God sees us, not the way we have been conditioned by others. If not, we can struggle with self-esteem or low self worth for a long time.

Thirdly, if we can connect with the concept of a Godly self-image, which translates in to a healthy self-esteem, we can then develop Godly self-confidence. However, if the first two are not complete then self-motivation is also affected: Many people try to hide and disguise this but it really does become apparent when the pressure is applied, or when circumstances challenge it. If you don't believe this, watch the behaviour of those who are put under pressure or who don't honour commitments, or even those who are late all the time and you will usually be able to trace this back to low Godly self image.

By way of contrast there are people and I'm sure you've met them, who seem almost over confident, even to the point of being arrogant. This kind of confidence usually isn't real, but rather it's more likely covering over some kind of insecurity. Whenever that person is lying down to sleep, on their own with nobody around – remember that is the person they really are, and I would suggest they are not as confident then as when in front of others.

Thank God our confidence is in Him and not people. As believers, it is so important that we have real confidence as we need this to deal with life's trials and challenges. This confidence begins with being comfortable with ourselves. We need to understand and catch our uniqueness. We can all look at other people sometimes wishing we were them. Well, guess what, we're not. If God wanted us to be them, he would have made us that way. Thankfully he made us to be just that – us, and we need to be comfortable with that.

As Christians, if we aren't whole ourselves, in a Godly sense, how then can we help others. Can hurting and wounded people help hurting and wounded people? Of course many people won't admit to being hurt and wounded. Some people's wounds are very visible and the pain is really quite raw. Others, for whatever reason have worked their way through their challenges to the point that the wounds aren't as visible, they're actually covered up quite well, yet some people still seek to be approved and recognised by men as if this will in some strange way change how they are valued. Unfortunately this is still an insecurity that only God can fill.

It's worth taking some time to look at this and to study what the word of God has to say on confidence, because the world is crying out for people who have real Godly based confidence, instead of the unhealthy kind which is so prevalent today, even in the church.

Chapter 4

Leading a disciplined life

I remember hearing someone say once 'if our relationship with God was based on how we feel, it would be up and down like a yo-yo!' That is so true.

I keep a feather in my Bible as a constant reminder that the Christian life is not easy, even though it is the only life worth living, full of hope and purpose. Why the feather? Well, if you stroke a feather there is a natural way it should be stroked. However, it is much more difficult to stroke it the other way, which is the way we live as believers and followers of Jesus, living out our lives on this earth.

Interestingly, being disciplined in life is a general requirement. For example, you need discipline for work and study, when to wake up, what to eat, what not to eat and on it goes. Yet, it's almost as if this same discipline doesn't need to be applied to our faith walk in the same way. If we lie on in bed (its usually warmer when it involves our faith), rather than get up to begin the day with the Lord and read his word, or we skip church because we don't feel like going, then that's ok. Well, faith is like a muscle, the more you exercise it the stronger it gets.

I heard a story of a man who had two dogs which he took bets on to fight each other. The man always seemed to come away from each fight winning all the money. Someone close to him eventually asked him how he was able to predict which dog would win the fight. He replied, 'the one I feed'

What we feed in our lives will be prominent, or as I said earlier 'what we give place to.'

> But I say, walk and live (habitually) in the (Holy) Spirit (responsive to and controlled and guided by the Spirit); then you will certainly not gratify the cravings and desires of the flesh (of human nature without God)

> Galatians 5: 16 (The Amplified Bible)

Have you ever arranged something early in the morning and when the alarm rings, you just cringe and decide to roll over again. I think we've all been there at one time or other. Apart from having just allowed the flesh to win, we have let someone down who has been depending on us. Instances like these and the lack of discipline in our lives can paint a clear picture of character to the point that it can become a flaw. Nobody wants to have a character flaw, but very often everyone else sees it except you. People quickly write you off as being unreliable or they say things to each other like, 'sure they're all talk and little else.' Don't be that person, beat the flesh and become a person of character.

The key word in the Amplified Version of Galatians 5 and 16 is 'habitually' and in this context can be translated disciplined. However, even though we are commanded continually to live our lives towards God and seek to be righteous and holy, we are still human. Whenever we do slip or fail God in some way, and we all do, we move away from his best for us. That said, we always have a tendency to look at our own failings differently from others. It is amazing how many times people openly comment about the sins or failings of others, forgetting that they had done exactly the same at one time in their life. Also, the more prominent the person, the more we amplify the failing. We begin to move dangerously towards the league table of sin and this of course is always based on our own value system, or our own pet hates, we will talk more about this in a later chapter.

One thing is certain, when we fail God we should feel remorseful and our conscience and the Holy Spirit within us, will challenge our ways. The dangerous place is when we willingly continue a sinful behaviour even when we are being challenged by the Holy Spirit. If we persist along this path, ultimately we will move off course and get to a place where we can justify our sin to ourselves. That is exactly where satan wants us to be.

Overcoming the flesh

Some of the most memorable times in my Christian life have been when I have fought the flesh, in other words doing something you absolutely 'don't feel' like doing.

I remember one night a number of years ago when I met with a group of guys who were struggling with issues in their lives brought about mostly by alcohol and drugs. I always arranged the meeting time quite late as my sons were younger at the time and I liked to get them to bed first. I was really tired and felt like calling and cancelling.

However, I forced myself out (which is always the most difficult part) and went on to see God move in amazing ways. It is really quite humbling when this happens particularly after not really wanting to go that night.

Also, on the way home that night, it was really late and I admit I was driving faster than I should have as I just wanted to get home. It had been raining heavily all day and as I approached a hill I heard this voice say "Slow down now"

I immediately braked and as I drove over the hill I saw the whole road submerged in water. I thank God he warns us and protects us when we need him.

I remember thinking that none of that would have happened if I had allowed my flesh to win that evening.

As Christians we take the flesh test every day in some way or another. It usually challenges our self control. As I write this I am reminded of a situation in business when a really irate customer was on the phone venting off about a mistake that had been made. After trying to fend the customer off my secretary passed the call through to me. As I took the call I remember seeing heads slowly rising to look in the window to see how I was going to deal with the customer. Would I engage in a shouting match or would I keep calm? Well, the truth is, in this instance I was simply honest, and yes, I admit I my ears were ringing a little afterwards, but that was ok.

As believers 'we are our neighbour's Bible, they read us every day.'

Being disciplined means overcoming the flesh, there is no easy way. Training the spirit, body and soul in the ways of the Lord will produce results that will open doors that no man can shut. Remember God knows when we win or lose the flesh battle.

Chapter 5

The power of prayer

T his is a most important part of the Christian life yet when the word prayer is mentioned it often triggers different responses from believers. Some get really excited while others seem to look bored. Has someone ever asked you to pray for them and of course you say you will, and don't. Have you ever been challenged to pray and didn't? Go on, be honest!!

The following story reinforces the importance of being obedient when we're prompted to pray:

A missionary home for a period of rest told this story while visiting his home church.

"While serving at a small field hospital in Africa, every two weeks I travelled by bicycle through the jungle to a nearby city for supplies. This was a journey of two days and required camping overnight at the halfway point.

On one of these journeys, I arrived in the city where I planned to collect money from a bank, purchase medicine, and supplies, and then begin my two-day journey back to the field hospital.

Upon arrival in the city, I observed two men fighting, one of whom had been seriously injured. I treated him for his injuries and at the same time talked to him about the Lord.

I then travelled two days, camping overnight, and arrived home without incident. . .

Two weeks later I repeated my journey.

Upon arriving in the city, I was approached by the young man I had treated. He told me that he had known I carried money and medicines. He said, 'Some friends and I followed you into the jungle, knowing you would camp overnight. We planned to kill you and take your money and drugs.

But just as we were about to move into your camp, we saw that you were surrounded by 26 armed guards.

At this, I laughed and said that I was certainly all alone in that jungle campsite.

The young man pressed the point, however, and said, 'No, sir, I was not the only person to see the guards, my friends also saw them, and we all counted them. It was because of those guards that we were afraid and left you alone.'

At this point in the sermon, one of the men in the congregation jumped to his feet and interrupted the missionary and asked if he could tell him the exact day this happened.

The missionary told the congregation the date and the man who interrupted told him this story:

"On the night of your incident in Africa, it was morning here and I was preparing to go play golf. I was about to putt when I felt the urge to pray for you. In fact, the urging of the Lord was so strong; I called men in this church to meet with me here in the sanctuary to pray for you. Would all of those men who met with me on that day stand up?"

The men who had met together to pray that day stood up. The missionary wasn't concerned with who they were, he was too busy counting how many men he saw.

There were 26!

This story is an incredible example of how the Spirit of the Lord moves in mysterious ways.

There are people who think nothing of taking hours in prayer. They can wake up in the middle of the night and spend the early hours interceding for whoever the Lord puts on their heart. I must say I'm personally not like that. I find myself talking to God first thing in the morning and at different times through the course of a day, depending on what I'm doing. I'm not the type of person you should ask something important to after 10pm at night, as I have already shut down for the night.

Personal prayer

As a husband and a father I thank God I met him and trusted him early enough to understand my responsibility as head of a home. It is my daily responsibility to take my family before the throne of God in prayer. Now, that sounds rather holy, but trust me, as a believer of many years I know the importance of this. Rather than sounding religious with man-made rules and conditions, I would simply say, culti-vate a lifestyle of prayer and pray often for your family and others as you are led by the Holy Spirit.

Do not fret or have any anxiety about anything, but in every circumstance and in everything, by prayer and petition (definite requests) with thanksgiving, continue to make your wants known to God.

Philippians Chapter 4 verse 6 (The Amplified Bible)

You don't need to be regarded as a special intercessor to pray for others when you are prompted to. I can list countless times when I have felt the urgency to pray for specific people and situations. That doesn't mean that I needed to pray for a certain length of time. You generally know when it is finished.

Pray at all times (on every occasion, in every season) in the spirit, with all (manner of) prayer and entreaty. To that end keep alert and watch with strong purpose and perseverance, interceding in behalf of all the saints (God's consecrated people).

Ephesians Chapter 6 verse 18 (The Amplified Bible)

It's also worth mentioning there are likely to be many times we don't feel like praying. Interestingly, that is the very time when our prayer is needed. The devil seeks to use circumstances to make sure we don't feel worthy, or in the mood for prayer. The same kind of thing usually happens when we are getting ready to go to church. The devil is cunning and thinks if he succeeds in stopping us from praying he has won. He is wrong of course. Break through by beginning to declare the word of God and praising the name of Jesus and you will get to the place of prayer much quicker.

Corporate prayer

As much as personal prayer is a lifestyle, corporate prayer or meeting with other believers is extremely important. It gives God great joy when believers meet together in unity. When we come together to pray I'm always amazed at how this special time can quickly bring us together in spirit, in one accord. The speed of life makes sure that believers come together with their minds full of the events of the day. Yet, when some time is spent in worship we begin to develop that expectancy that only comes from Jesus.

A memorable instance in my life was a night when a group I was involved with, met to pray for those in need. It was clear that the day had been stressful for many of us in the room for one reason or other. It would have been easy to start and almost go through the motions by praying from our heads and not from our hearts. There is a real difference.

I felt before we began to pray we should take time sharing with each other about the events of the day and we found ourselves beginning to encourage each other by talking about times when God answered prayer. Before long there was an atmosphere of faith in the room and it was time to pray. That night God met us powerfully and answered prayer in a mighty way. One situation that really amazed me was how God changed a person's behaviour overnight, halfway around the world. I still remember thinking that the God of the universe is powerful and that I shouldn't limit him to answering a prayer in my time zone.

God is truly amazing and His ways are above my ways.

Faith filled prayers

The Lord is clear in scripture when it comes to prayer. The Bible says that the prayer of the righteous man makes great spiritual power available. We have been given everything we need and this extends to prayer. One of the more controversial passages is in the book of Matthew. Jesus speaking to his disciples said:

Because of the littleness of your faith (that is, your lack of firmly relying trust) for truly I say to you, if you have faith (that is living) like a grain of mustard seed, you can say to this mountain. Move from here to yonder place, and it will move; and nothing will be impossible to you

Matthew 17 verse 20 (The Amplified Bible)

I say controversial in that many believers find it difficult to accept this verse in its entirety. One thing is certain, the instruction from Jesus is clear, he says "you can say" if you exercise faith. Now there are occasions when it seems prayer is not answered, but that really isn't enough reason to stop believing for the impossible.

It's beyond me to understand the 'whys' and 'why nots' of this life, but I simply cannot quit praying for the needy, those in need of miracles, because God still moves in signs and wonders today on the earth and I always don't have to look too far back to a time when God last answered my prayer.

The Authority of the Believer

The Bible says we do not fight against natural, physical opponents:

For we are not wrestling with flesh and blood (contending only with physical opponents) but against the despotisms, against the powers, against (the master spirits, who are) the world rulers of this present darkness, against the spirit forces of wickedness in the heavenly (supernatural) sphere

Ephesians Chapter 6 verse 12 (The Amplified bible)

Can you picture a great crowd of people gathered together and let's say for example, the president of a country begins to approach the crowd. Automatically, the people make way for the president and a pathway opens up before him. By way of contrast, imagine an ordinary person approaching the same crowd; they have to push their way through as no way is opening before them.

I believe it's the same way in the spiritual realm. There is a clear awareness in the spiritual realm as to who carries Godly authority.

Consider this account in the book of Acts:

13. Then some of the travelling Jewish exorcists (men who adjure evil spirits) also undertook to call the name of Lord Jesus over those who had evil spirits, saying, I solemnly implore and charge you by the Jesus whom Paul preaches!

14. Seven sons of a certain Jewish Chief Priest named Sceva were doing this.

15. But (one) evil spirit retorted, Jesus I know, and Paul I know about, but who are you?

16. Then the man in whom the evil spirit dwelt leaped upon them, mastering two of them, and was so violent against them that they dashed out of that house (in fear), stripped naked and wounded.

Acts Chapter 19 verses 13 to 16 (The Amplified Bible)

The message of this passage is clear and poses an important question, 'are we known to the forces of darkness as a believer with authority?' If we were to approach a crowd in the spiritual context would it open up before us, recognising something of the authority we carry? Or would we be like the ordinary person pushing through a crowd?

That is our challenge and as we go to prayer we should always ensure we are prepared and know where our feet are, not on soft ground, but standing on the rock, Christ Jesus.

A while ago my wife and I received a telephone call late in the evening from a couple who were distressed. They lived in a house where a so-called Ghost or a familiar spirit was causing some disruption. This figure had been appearing at different times and obviously the family weren't sleeping too well at all, as I'm sure you could imagine. This, along with a few other issues had really upset this couple and they asked if we would visit them and pray.

Well, it was late in the evening and my flesh didn't like the idea of setting out at this time of night to the place which was about an hour's drive from our house. However, we called a friend to join us and set off to visit them. The reason I am telling this is that I believe it was a true test of authority. As I drove to the house, I was extremely aware of the forces of darkness that were in operation. If I was not in a place where I understood and was practicing my spiritual authority, I would have been better off turning the car around and driving back home.

We arrived at the house, met the folk and prayed. We walked around the entire place inside and out, anointed the doors and windows with oil as a symbol of the power of Jesus Christ. I must say that I did sense evil as I walked through the house, but praise God the result was that the couple were able to sleep soundly from that night on.

Remember an important fact here 'We have nothing to fear from the forces of evil, providing we know whom we have believed and are walking with the Lord Jesus Christ every day, giving him central place in our lives.

There are many Christians who are frightened of the devil's power and the forces of evil, almost convinced that this is way out of their league. It's really worth emphasising that every believer qualifies and has authority in Jesus Christ through his blood that was shed for us. All we need to do is to begin to exercise that authority. There's no greater power on this earth than the name of Jesus Christ, now that's something to give thanks for.

Chapter 6

Our walk talks

'That you would walk worthy of God who calls you into his own kingdom and glory'

1 Thessalonians 2:12 NKJV

Whether we like it or not, in this Christian life we are people of influence. Our walking actually does do the talking.

I remember hearing the story of a young man who had finished his studies and went to visit a wise old mentor figure. He said, 'I've finished all my studies and education, what do you think I should do? What do you think the world needs?

The old man replied, 'Son, you're asking the wrong question, you should be asking yourself, what makes you come alive?' Find out what that is, and go do it, because what the world needs, is people who have come alive.

That story really stayed with me and I have referred to it many times when talking to people about their lives and direction. The experts (whoever they are) tell us that even the most introverted person will influence 10,000 people in a life time. That's talking about someone who is extremely shy and withdrawn. The average person, therefore, is likely to influence many more than that. Remember, we are maybe the only Jesus some people will see.

A friend of mine was on an intensive training course with around 20 others for a number of weeks. On the first day they were all gathered in a room and each was asked to tell the group a little about themselves, usual kind of thing. When it came to my friend's time he began to talk about his life and said that he was a Christian.

He went on to say that he didn't want to be treated any differently, even though some of the language and coarse joking would not be his choice and that he looked forward to getting to know others over the next few weeks they would be together.

Later on that day, three others came to him and whispered that they were Christians too but didn't feel bold enough to mention it and admired him for doing so. My friend earned some respect from the group that day which resulted in him having some great opportunities to talk about his faith to others during his time there.

As a young Christian, I learned that when in the company of non-believers, it is much better to let them know your stance early, without preaching it to them, as it is much more difficult to do so later.

Wouldn't it be great if a row of people were lined up and it included both Christians and non-Christians and you were able to physically see the difference; something in the countenance of the believer that stood out from the crowd, prompting people to say 'there's something different about them.' I firmly believe that this should be our challenge 'all' of the time.

As believers, most of the time we're in the minority wherever we go, therefore it's more important than ever that we allow the presence of God, through the Holy Spirit to be visible to others. Have you ever been somewhere and someone curses, looks at you and apologises? This has happened to me a number of times and I don't believe they knew that I was a believer.

I made a decision some years ago that I would try to start a conversation with whoever I met, whether on a plane, in a waiting room etc. This has been my opportunity to use my influence to show the love and compassion of Christ to those I meet. Of course I don't always feel like it and there have been times where it has been very brief, but I believe it is a good practice and I have had some memorable opportunities along the way. We should remember though that when we meet strangers, an encouraging or challenging word may impact them significantly after we're gone. One word from God can change a life forever, we need to realise He may deliver that word through us!

There is a powerful song birthed by a group in Northern Ireland called 'The God of the City.' In the song it puts very well the role we have as believers in our circle of influence.

It says we bring light to the darkness, hope to the hopeless and peace to the restless. What a job of influence we have.

Have you ever been to a function and there are lots of folks standing around waiting for the function to begin, everybody looks around at each other awkwardly looking for either someone they know, or at least someone who looks approachable. A smile is easily carried and you usually feel attracted to someone with a warm smiling face rather than one you could hang your coat on.

Preach the gospel and if necessary use words

I heard a story once from a guy who wasn't a Christian and worked in a large factory. Amongst the rough talking men were a few fellows who were 'religious.' By the way, that description really bothers me as it describes something that is man-made and doesn't really explain what a true Christian is. It's worth noting that someone who is 'religious', i.e. goes to church, and reads the Bible may actually be different from a true Christian. A true Christian is one who has given their entire life over to Jesus Christ, trusting him to lead and direct them, giving them the strength to follow as closely as they can to the best example of living known to man. That's not to say they're perfect, that person hasn't been born yet, but let's be clear, it's up to God at the end of time to decide who is who, as the Bible tells us that we must give account for our lives on earth. If that doesn't humble us, nothing will.

Anyway, according to the non-Christian in the factory, there were two guys he watched closely. One was really loud about his faith and seemed to push his views on others, pulling them up for language and leaving tracts around. He always sat in a corner reading his Bible at break times. The other was a quieter guy, the type who was helpful and always encouraging those around him. He could have a laugh and visited if someone was off sick. He lent his car to someone if they needed to go somewhere urgently. People seemed to chat to him when they had a problem.

The moral of the story is this, 'we can influence people either positively or negatively' and as believers that is something we must take seriously. We have a duty to make God attractive to those we come in contact with.

I learned this very powerfully whilst running a company a few years ago.

A succession of customers and suppliers came to me over a period of a couple of weeks, complaining about how they were being treated by 'so called Christians.' In one instance, a supplier, whom I had got to know well over a number of years, had arranged to call and collect a cheque from a Christian businessman and he received three cheques, two of which were post dated. By the time the supplier had returned, his office had received a call advising them not to lodge the cheques as there wouldn't be sufficient funds to cover them. My supplier asked me, knowing my stance as a Christian, what I would do?

I told him that I would be present at the guy's church the next week and challenge his behaviour in front of those he clearly acted differently around, as this example was clearly unacceptable and painted a poor picture of Christianity to this supplier. I'm not sure if this was the right thing to do or not, or even whether I would have carried it through, but I remember that particular period of time being really disillusioned for a time, until I realised I got a revelation - I wasn't responsible for them. They would have to answer for themselves some-day. Again I say we must take seriously our responsibility as Christians as we may be the only Jesus people see. He will either be portrayed as attractive through our actions and lives or he won't - it's that simple.

Chapter 7

Healthy relationships

L ife is full of examples of how 'not' to do relationships. We are often inclined to look at the so-called role models in all the wrong settings. Obviously this is more common nowadays through media such as reality TV, films and glossy magazines.

I remember thinking a lot about this during my time as a youth pastor. Just how young people form relationships is amazing, never mind older folks. When I think about the 'relate' part in the word relationship, it brings me back to the times when I took groups of young people to the mountains for activity type weekends. Whenever we arrived, the first thing we did was organise the sleeping arrangements, male and female separate of course. It was amazing to see how those from broken homes and single parent backgrounds seemed to be drawn to each other. They 'related' to each other yet often they didn't even know each other.

The many relationships in life can range from casual to close friendship. They include working relationships, and of course there is the romantic kind. Looking at these differing types of relationships from a Christian perspective, the first thing we should realise is that making sensible choices has a great deal to do with the success of any relationship. What do I mean? Well, there are those who will pull you down in life, and there are those who will build you up. There are encouragers and discouragers. There are those who are openly for you, and those who are quietly against you. Of course there are times when you have little choice but to be with folks and have a relationship with them, the workplace being a good example and these relationships require wisdom. However, there are other more emotionally driven relationships where we need to exercise caution.

When young people get to the time in their lives when they begin to see the opposite sex as attractive, they move into dangerous territory. I say this because hormones were not designed with brakes. Therefore it is actually very important that young people are taught how to set boundaries, and not let the heat of a moment ruin their lives. Sadly, Christian parents are divided on this subject, some are very liberal, particularly with younger sons and daughters, allowing them to dress and keep company with friends as they like, without having any real idea where they are and what they are doing. Others are more definite in what they approve of, setting clear ground rules and keeping them tight. Either way, children and young people only have one life, and the choices they make will determine their course.

Parenting is much more difficult nowadays due to the breakdown of the family unit and the never ending peer pressure brought about by friends.

The order has been set for all us; children are the responsibility of parents. It's not for others to lead our children, and let's be honest; there are plenty who would try.

I believe we have a growing responsibility to the young people of today, whether they are our immediate sons and daughters or not. We should be setting an example for them to follow, we should be able to relate to them and help them when they need guidance. This includes speaking godly truths to them in a non judgemental way. What needs to be said usually needs to be said, but the way it's said can often be the problem.

I spoke to a young girl recently who was introduced to me by her friend. She was 17 years old and had a baby of 9 months old. She and the baby's father were not together and the girl depended on her mother to help with the baby. My heart really felt for her as she told me how she felt condemned by what had happened, yet here was a young girl with her whole life ahead of her. If ever anyone needs to have healthy relationships in her life, she does.

In the days ahead this girl needs positive role models of both sexes who will encourage her to grow into a godly young woman and mother, impacting her generation. This life is for living, not enduring:

> The thief comes only in order to steal, kill and destroy. I (Jesus) came that they may have and enjoy life, and have it in abundance (to the full, till it overflows)
>
> John Chapter 10 verse 10 (The Amplified Bible)

We have a duty as believers to be fathers to the fatherless, and this may push us outside of our comfort zone at times, but it may be absolutely vital for someone in our circle of influence.

> And he will reply to them. Solemnly I declare to you, in so far as you failed to do it for the least (in the estimation of men) of these, you failed to do it for me.
>
> Matthew 25 verse 45 (The Amplified Bible)

The marriage relationship

Even though marriage seems to be coming less popular today, with more people living together, marriage is God's plan for Christians who come together as man and wife. There is no other way for the Christian. I can speak with the experience of someone who was married at 20 years of age and that was well over 25 years ago. One thing I learned from being married young was that I didn't have it all worked out. I would honestly say that our marriage is like what's said of a good wine; it has matured and got better with age.

There are many different situations and pressures that married people face. Some of these are work related or financial, others include kids coming quickly into the relationship and the challenges they present. Of course there are extras like church, sport, other hobbies and not to be forgotten, the in-laws. This combination can make for a busy life.

However, there are a number of important keys to a healthy marriage relationship, some of these are probably known to you, but beware, they require working out. I speak from the experience of knowing these, but not really understanding the importance of them until I was married for a number of years. Unfortunately there are usually consequences when they slip. Through my life experience I've come to realise that some things are important and the following points are what I've learned most:

1.

As Christians, invite and learn to keep Christ at the centre of your marriage. Take all important decisions to him in prayer. Also if you are a Christian man, become the head of the home, if not already, according to scripture, not as a tyrant, but as a loving husband and father, keeping sight of God's grace, and depending on His wisdom for every decision.

2.

Reserve a generous amount of time to communicate with each other and try not to let the busy schedule break this. The reason so many marriages grow cold is because talking has become limited to a few words at the dinner table and discussions over the children, or money matters with little time left for genuine conversation.

3.

Take time to understand that men are men, and women are women. We are made differently. What is important to a woman is often not important to a man and vice versa. I probably found this out the hard way, but I'm getting better. I now know the importance of affirming one another, really letting your life partner know that you love them and believe in them. I have also realised the importance of giving a hand around the house rather than trying to ignore the request. That one was learned slowly and at times painfully!!

4.

When the kids come along, make sure you give as much time to them as possible. I know for many people, child-minding is a way of life due to work commitments, but a lot of life is lived outside of work.

Children don't want to be bought off with gifts, they want time. Spending time with your children rather than going off to do something else less important is a life lesson, which is usually learned too late.

Fathers, do not irritate and provoke your children to anger (do not exasperate them to resentment) but rear them (tenderly) in the training and discipline and the counsel and admonition of the Lord

Ephesians Chapter 6 verse 4 (The Amplified Bible)

Whenever the Bible talks about teaching and disciplining children, it's not referring to a correspondence course.

One thing I have heard more the older I've got is 'I wish I had spent more time with my children.' Sadly, Christians are often in this group and have somehow convinced themselves to believe other things are more important than being there for their children as they grow up.

If you don't agree with this, remember the look on your child's face when they pick you out in the crowd when taking part in a school play or a sporting event. That smile, the lingering look, enforces the role we have as godly parents.

Rob Parsons, of Care for the Family, told a story once about a father who took his son to the ice cream parlour after promising to do it for a while. Shortly after they got to the shop and sat down with the ice creams, the door opened and in came someone from the church. As the father was the church treasurer he said to his son, 'I'll be back in a minute' and went over to talk to the other person. After sitting for 10 minutes, the son went over to his dad and nudged him. His father reached him some money and sent him to get another ice cream. That was the end of the trip. Time went on and the years went by and the son got married and moved away.

One day the father rang his son and said 'Hello son, I was wondering if I could come down to see you?' The son replied, 'Sorry Dad, I'm rather busy at the moment, perhaps we can arrange it for another time!' The father came off the phone and after thinking a few moments, he remembered back to times like the ice-cream shop. He thought about how quickly life had moved on, oh, how he would have loved to be able to wind the clock back.

This story is real and it should remind us to seize the day, and not put off to tomorrow, something that we can do today, oh and by the way, nobody has ever been known to say on their death bed, 'I wish I spent more time at the office.'

Chapter 8

The Right Direction

Have you noticed just how many books are available these days about guidance? Self-help books are everywhere these days - the seven ways to discover this, and the five tips to becoming that. The concerning thing is, more and more people are buying them, yet, there are also so many people who seem to be wandering through life aimlessly, just drifting along the lazy river. Some want to find out life's direction but are looking in all the wrong places, others seem content to amble along in no particular direction.

Life shouldn't be like this. Every person has been given life to develop and grow, be effective in their generation, and above all, enjoy living as much as possible along the way, not enduring it. The Bible says life more 'abundantly.'

The thief does not come except to steal, and to kill, and to destroy. I have come that they may have life, and that they may have it more abundantly.

John 10:10 NKJV

Life is truly precious and we really need to grasp the fact that it's not a rehearsal, this is it. The Bible also says that without a vision the people perish. There is powerful truth in this statement.

I personally believe God always takes us the way of our gifts. A gift is something that is given to you. It's a faculty that has been miraculously bestowed upon you, so to speak. Have you ever asked yourself, 'Why would God, the Creator, give you a gift and not expect you to use it?' Imagine someone goes to great lengths to give you a gift, a present, and you set it in the corner and never use it. How would the giver feel if every time they visited you, they saw the gift lying in the corner unused?

We talk about gifts and talents in the same sentence most of the time, yet I like to think of talents slightly differently. A talent is about having an ability to do something. For example, a car mechanic, a carpenter, or accountant all have ability in their respective professions, but they all had to spend long hours, often being taught by others before they were considered talented. A gift, in the other hand is something you can do easily, almost with your eyes closed; you just do it naturally without even thinking about it.

Whether you agree with me that gifts are God given and talents are man-made, so to speak, or not, one thing is certain, they are likely to feature in your life's direction.

I have known quite a few people who have been coerced into something they don't enjoy doing for a number of reasons. It may be a family business, or a profession that the father did, therefore so should they; or it may have simply been a job opportunity that started as a stepping-stone but now seems like there's no way out. As someone once said 'if you look in the mirror more days in the week than not and say to yourself, 'I really don't want to go there today,' then you are probably just going through the motions and it's time to move on.

Many young people start down the road of university without giving any real thought to course suitability. They spend a couple of years and then change or quit all together.

As Christians we are guided simply from God's word on how to seek direction for our lives. Of course it's important to begin with understanding again how God looks at us, how He sees us, how we're made in His image, and how He only has the best in mind for us.

But seek (aim at and strive after) first of all his kingdom and his righteousness (his way of doing things and being right) and then all these things taken together will be given you besides

Matthew Chapter 6 verse 33 (The Amplified Version)

There is no doubt in my mind that this portion of scripture has wisdom written all over it. Another popular verse in the same vein is:

Lean on, trust in, and be confident in the Lord with all your heart and mind and do not rely on your own insight or understanding. In all your ways acknowledge him, and he will direct and make straight and plain your paths

Proverbs Chapter 3 verses 5 & 6 (The Amplified Version)

If we can apply these verses to our lives and focus on Jesus, He will begin to reveal his plan for us by opening up doors that we don't necessarily have to push. There will be others that we will know when to push. When we follow the command above, we'll know the difference.

I used to be the type of person who pushed doors so hard, they nearly came off the hinges. All I needed was the slightest hint that it may be the way, the thing to do, and off I went. Can I tell you, whenever I acted like that, things simply never worked out.

When I got hold of this scripture and focused on the kingdom first, then it started to change. I concentrated on doing whatever I had at my hand to do, not being idle, or waiting for God to drop something from the sky, I don't think that's what these verses mean, but simply doing what was in front of me at that time.

There are times in life when direction is clearer than others. When it's not so clear, our minds begin to race and we can dream up all kinds of stuff. 'Maybe I should do that, or maybe this is something I could be doing.' These times can be very confusing.

When this has happened to me, I write down the list of possible directions and keep them in my Bible. I then spend time meditating on the verses in Proverbs and every so often I look at the list. I've found myself being able to instantly rule out an option every time, until I have got rid of the confusion. This has really helped me keep the mind from racing along.

It says in the book of Proverbs:

A man's mind plans his way, but the Lord directs his steps and makes them sure

Proverbs Chapter 16 verse 9 (The Amplified Bible)

I remember a time in my life when I really thought I was going to be involved in a particular work assignment, in fact I would go as far as saying I was convinced. Did I get a word from the Lord on it? No, I didn't, but I felt sure there was something significant in it.

As I committed this to God and tried my best to leave it there, there was a 'suddenly' that happened. Before I knew it one day, I received a telephone call at 2.00pm with a new major opportunity, and at 3.00pm an email closing the door I thought would open.

The lesson I learned from this is that it's time to relax and begin to rest in God's presence when it comes to life's direction. If we seek Him first, and commit our ways to Him, He says that He will never leave nor forsake us, surely that should be enough.

Chapter 9

Seven Days a Week

I've heard Christian people say 'I just live for Sundays.' As they are speaking, I'm thinking, 'What about the rest of the week then?' Whether it's school, university, the factory, the office, public service, business etc, or even if you're reading this and you are unemployed for one reason or the other, this place is your ministry place also. It's almost as if work or study is kind of getting in the way and obstructing what could otherwise be an ideal life.

There is a myth that exists in the body of Christ or among Christians today, that you haven't quite made it as a Christian until you get to this place called 'full-time ministry.' Once you become 'full time' you have made it into the 'hall of fame' so to speak.

What does the term 'ministry' really mean?

The traditional meaning is usually referring to clergy, or the profession and duties of a minister, pastor or priest.

The more modern day meaning refers more to acts of service, implying that we are all in ministry, that is the work of the Lord, but the terminology has become confusing and misleading.

My view on this is very simple, as Christians, we are in ministry wherever we take Jesus. If we choose to allow His presence in our lives only in the church setting, then that is where our ministry extends. However, if we allow Jesus to accompany us every day on life's journey, then we are in full time ministry.

The 'full time' theory can also be encouraged for example, if you are part of a vibrant outreaching church or ministry, where your passion for the work can find you convincing yourself that if you weren't spending as much time working, you could dedicate more time to the ministry or church work.

I personally don't hold that view. As much as I believe there is a definite call to ministry in a full time work capacity, i.e. working for a church or ministry all week every week, it is not for the majority of Christians. Yes of course we need ministers, pastors and staff members who are employed by the church to help get the work done, but most of us are not called in this way. We are however called to our own specific circle of influence. Yes, we can volunteer our time and our skills for the benefit of Church ministry and that is so important, but it's the school, university, factory, and office or wherever our profession takes us, that we are called to live out our faith.

We can either choose to look on this as a chore or a privilege, yet because it's work, we're more likely to see it as a necessary evil to make some money. If we think about work as putting in the time, it really does get boring and pointless. Every day is set before us with opportunity; when we hold this view, everything changes. Our work or workplace may well be our life assignment for Jesus.

Also, the church and its work usually needs people to help provide finance for all its activities and ministries of help to the community. How would it flourish if everybody became full-time in the church?

God's people are required everywhere, living out the principles of Christianity in the workplace. We need people with high morals and godly wisdom and influence in the marketplace, and in society in general. I think back to the time when my children started school. I really saw just how much influence a teacher has in the life of a child in its formative years. Consider politics for example, or other government agencies, and think again just how important it is that Christians have a say in decision making at the highest level.

This is the place where the example of the believer is so very important, that we would become known as people of wisdom and influence.

My work has taken me into various companies and organisations, often as an interim manager and non-executive director. I remember sitting at a board meeting one day where a very delicate and serious issue was being debated.

Someone asked what my view was, and what I thought should be done. All of a sudden, all the heads leaned forward and looked down the table towards me, waiting for me to answer. At that precise moment, I realised that every word I would speak required God's wisdom. It really let me see how much influence we have as believers. Unfortunately we sometimes just don't see it.

As an interim manager, part of the challenge is taking charge of an organisation for a specific time during a period of change. I remember again whilst on assignment, once having to address a large workforce and walking out to a sea of faces waiting nervously for what I had to say. Again, this memory reminds me of the awesome privilege and responsibility of having the opportunity to lead in business.

God has given us the ability to be among the leaders of our nation, and in all walks of life. We have the duty to grow and develop ourselves, always learning more.

A few years ago I set myself the challenge that every year I would undertake training relating to my faith and business. So I look to attend a Christian course and a business course annually in order to sharpen my understanding. I'm really glad I set myself this challenge as it has really kept me focused and motivated to influence more, encourage more and stretch more as I deal with life's challenges.

Chapter 10

When Trials Come

The New International Version of the Bible says in James Chapter 1

Consider it pure joy, my brothers whenever you face trials of many kinds, because you know that the testing of your faith develops perseverance. Perseverance must finish its work so that you may become mature and complete, not lacking anything

James Chapter 1 verse 2 (New International Version)

Whenever I first began to study this passage and trials being referred to as 'pure joy', it really jarred my thinking because they usually felt the opposite. The older I get, however, I believe this reference makes more sense.

The Message translation puts it this way:

Consider it a sheer gift friends, when tests and challenges come at you from all sides. You know that under pressure, your faith life is forced out into the open and shows its true colours. So don't try and get out of anything prematurely. Let it do its work so you become mature and well-developed, not deficient in any way

James Chapter 1 verse 2 (The Message Translation)

Isn't it amazing how people can show their true colours when trial or real crisis comes along. Some folks who have ridiculed the Christian life and have made fun of faith for years, all of a sudden become interested in what you and I believe. They ask you to pray for their situation and often admit they have even begun to pray themselves. Other 'luke-warm' Christians, open the drawer and bring God back out again, having put him away after their last crisis ended. Even those who are considered mature Christians can really wobble when the crisis and testing times come to visit. Regardless of the category, each and every person will have to deal with trials and crisis in their lives.

Some people have had to deal with horribly painful and shocking events that seem to be completely without reason or explanation, they just happen. It becomes a true test of faith for the person or families affected.

The Bible says, they overcame by the blood of the lamb and the word of their testimony, Revelation chapter 12, and verse 11. As Christians, we often have to undergo a test before we have a testimony. In fact as believers, it's usually first the test, then the testimony.

These challenging times can often be brought about by illness, death, financial trouble or unemployment. It's at times like these, the mind races in all directions, asking hard questions and finding few answers. It can be a lonely time for any person. Some people do the strangest things when those around them are going through crisis. Well-meaning folk come out with the most insensitive and stupid remarks, rather than just coming alongside those in the trial, simply being there for them in their time of need.

Rather than being unsure of what to say to those going through a trial, why not simply offer an act of kindness, a gift, a card, a meal, or even some money slipped through the letter box. Any of these are appreciated by someone going through trial, probably more than we will ever know.

The good news is that God brings peace to the troubled heart.

The Christian faith is the only faith that binds up the broken hearted. It's at times like these when the heart requires genuine comfort, and the faithfulness of God is the only real place of refuge. People may fail and change, but God never fails to provide through His Word and by the Holy Spirit. True comfort comes only from the supernatural Word of God.

Cast your burden on the Lord (releasing the weight of it) and he will sustain you. He will never allow the (consistently) righteous to be moved (made to slip, fall, or fail)

Psalm 55 & Verse 22 (The Amplified Bible)

The following story really demonstrates the faithfulness of God.

One tribe of native Americans had a unique practice for training young braves. On the night of the boy's thirteenth birthday, he was placed in a dense forest to spend the entire night alone. Until then he had never been away from the security of his family and tribe. But on this night he was blindfolded and taken miles away. When he took off the blindfold, he was in the middle of thick woods, by himself, all night long.

Every time a twig snapped, he probably visualised a wild animal ready to pounce. Every time the wind blew, he wondered what more sinister sound it masked. No doubt it was a terrifying night for many.

After what seemed like an eternity, the first rays of sunlight entered the interior of the forest. Looking around, the boy saw flowers, trees and the outline of the path. Then, to his utter astonishment, he beheld the figure of a man standing just a few feet away, armed with a bow and arrow. It was the boy's father. He had been there all night long.

Can you think of any better way for a child to learn how God allows us to face the tests of life? God is always present with us. God's presence is unseen, but it is more real than life itself.

Citation, Leonard Sweet, SoulSalsa (Zonderman 2000) pp 23-24 submitted by Mike Kjergaard, Hampton, Virginia

Trials of the people kind

Dealing with difficult people can also be a testing place for the believer. Although there are those who would say they have no problem dealing with confrontation, I have yet to meet anyone who enjoys it. I learned a valuable lesson in this area early in my Christian life.

It was late on a Friday afternoon in a company where I worked. Another manager and I had a heated exchange about something.

It took place in a fairly public place and anyone watching would have known from the body language that it was a disagreement. Anyhow, we were interrupted and had to leave it to deal with something else. I came home bubbling and simmering and tried to get the thing out of my head for the weekend. Before I knew what was happening, I began to think about it again and found myself planning a rematch. It was likely that we would resume this on Monday morning as it was unfinished business, so to speak. At different times throughout the weekend my imagination ran away with me, and on Monday morning, I found myself having a full blown argument with the guy in my head, even before I got out of bed.

As I drove to work that morning, I was rehearsing 'if he says that, I'll say this' and on it went, all in my mind of course.

I entered my workplace and there he was, standing at the end of a corridor. I started walking towards him with my heart beating louder, getting ready for action. As I approached him he held out his hand and said 'listen, I'm sorry about Friday, it was my fault.' I was speechless, no words came, and I simply smiled, thanked him and walked on.

I learned a valuable life lesson that day. The mind is an amazing thing and imagination is dangerous at times. All through the weekend I had allowed my mind and imagination to race along and blow the situation completely out of proportion. How stupid I was. The Bible helps us understand how to deal with this kind of trial:

We demolish arguments and every pretension that sets itself up against the knowledge of God, and we take captive every thought to make it obedient to Christ.

2 Corinthians 10 verse 5 (New International Version)

The advice given here in Corinthians is good, but it requires some practice. To take every thought captive at times when the mind would race, is difficult, but it works when we make them obedient to Christ. I have found from experience that this gets easier the more I do it.

Many confrontations or difficult people situations however, are unplanned, just like the example I gave. They just happen out of nowhere. One particular incident I remember happened when I was running a company where we were involved in supplying products which included fitting them on customer premises. I was in the office one day when another member of staff came in and signalled me to come with him. He had a customer on the phone that was cursing and swearing about a job we were doing on his premises.

We put him on the open phone and I entered the conversation. It didn't take very long to realise that this matter was not going to be solved by a phone call, as the customer was being abusive, loud and completely unreasonable. I closed the call by saying that I was leaving to drive directly to see him, and we would sort the problem out in person. Immediately I set off on what was just over a 1 hour drive, and of course began to rehearse the situation over in my mind.

I arrived at the premises, a new building full of all kinds of trades working to finish in time for a grand opening. As I entered the main door it reminded me of one of those old western movies at the saloon. Every one stopped and looked around at me and all of a sudden the noise ceased. I looked across and I saw my staff clearly under pressure. The next thing I knew, I heard these footsteps coming across the top floor and this voice at the top of the stairs bellowed, 'So you're the guy.'

The next thing I knew, this man started into a barrage of abuse shouting and yelling as he went. I signalled him to stop, and after about the third attempt got him to shut up. I then calmly (I really surprised myself) said to him that I had come to sort the matter out. Again he began to shout, and I stopped him, repeating that I had come to sort the matter out. Meanwhile everybody was standing around watching this live show with great amusement.

Finally, my customer accepted my offer of resolving the problem, which turned out to be nothing more than a simple misunderstanding.

I have learned some tips from this, and other experiences (the hard way) through life. They have really helped me deal with difficult people in a way that doesn't compromise my Christian values:

Don't take things personally

The other person dislikes confrontation as much as you do

Remember that whoever crosses over the point of reason will usually have to return.

If this happens, challenge the other person about becoming unreasonable

Don't allow things to get heated with raised voices. If it heads in this direction, shut it down and arrange to meet again later when tempers have cooled down

I was involved in a business once where one of the directors was known for being very difficult to work with. He had a very short fuse and had difficulty in controlling his temper.

We talked about this one day and I remember being amazed at him saying, the only confrontations he remembered were the ones where the other person kept their cool. Those who matched him blow for blow, shouting and roaring, he didn't remember.

Financial trials

When we follow the Lord in every area there are often times when we are stretched financially. It's at times like this we move into natural mode where we think, unless we can make it work, we can't see it happen. Our God is our provider even when we can't see it. There comes a point when either we believe in His abundant provision and refuse to be moved by events and circumstances around us, or we don't. Even in times where we have perhaps been unwise with our finances, when we ask God to forgive us and repent for being poor stewards, then He forgives and moves on our behalf. That word 'repent' means to turn around and go in the other direction. We often talk about this course of action when we decide to trust the Lord for the first time, but it's worth thinking about this in the context of poor stewardship and submitting to a lifestyle of debt.

Debt is buying something you want, that you can't afford. So when God helps out financially, try to get out of debt and live free from this in the future. The day you take the decision to get out of debt, prepare to be tested. Things may seem to tighten further making you think that the idea is too difficult. The enemy Satan, likes to keep people in this place, so tell him to go to where he belongs and break free today in the mighty name of Jesus.

Remember that circumstances are only the circle in which we stand. We can look out, step out and speak the word of God over our situations. Yes there are times when it doesn't look good, or there seems no way it can work out. In our natural eyes that it true, but we are not moved by what we see, we are moved and inspired by what we believe. The enemy Satan is often quick to whisper doubt and defeat in our ears. He wants us to panic and worry, he wants us to become so desperate that we go and do something crazy. He is defeated and we have the power through our words to combat the devil and dismiss him and his army from our lives.

I firmly believe if we live our lives according to the principles and Word of God, then he is duty bound to look after us. When we give generously and tithe our finances, when we live right and pure, setting the example Jesus himself has laid down, we will always have enough and the words of Psalm 91 will ring in our ear, then no harm will befall him and no disaster will come near his tent.

Chapter 11

The Gift of Encouragement

A few years ago when running a business I had a customer I remember clearly. I recall looking forward to him visiting as it had been almost a year since he was last with us. As he got out of his car I noticed he was walking with a limp. After a while, I asked him about the limp. He rolled up the leg of his trousers to uncover an artificial limb. He smiled and replied 'I had a disagreement with a JCB digger and it won.' I was shocked as I hadn't expected anything as serious.

I asked him how he dealt with having a leg amputated above the knee. He said 'I have good days and bad days.' What do you do on the bad days?' I asked. He replied, 'I get into the car and drive to the hospital where I had the operation, I walk through the ward and talk to the patients. When I come back out, I feel much better.'

This story reminds me how important the medicine of encouragement actually is. My wife's uncle once told us that whenever he feels down, he writes letters of encouragement to some folks he hasn't been in touch with for a while and immediately begins to feel much better, there is a clear principle at work here.

When was the last time you really encouraged some-body? I mean going out of your way and interrupting your schedule to really encourage someone who could do with it. I'm not necessarily talking about Christians; encouragement is something that is universal.

Some years ago, I read in the newspaper that my old rugby team were to play an important match, which if they won, meant they would win the league, quite an achieve-ment for the club as it had been quite a few years since this had happened. I decided to go and watch the match and at half time my team were getting beaten quite easily. A few old colleagues and I agreed to go the side of the pitch and encourage them during the second half. We began to shout and will them on to win, even in what seemed like an impossible situation. The look on their faces was quite something, even though the younger guys didn't really know us. However, they felt obligated to raise their game as we continued to tell them we believed in them, that they could do it. The turnaround was truly remarkable. My old team won that day.

It's good practice to encourage, why not embrace this as a lifestyle. I'm quite sure that if we really catch this and begin to encourage someone every day, the Lord will use this attitude of heart to draw others to him.

I want them to be encouraged and knit together by strong ties of love. I want them to have complete confidence that they understand God's mysterious plan, which is Christ himself

Colossians 2 verse 2 (The New Living Bible)

I remember talking to an under pressure company director one day and found myself encouraging him for about 5 min-utes or so. In that time he physically changed, responding to this encouragement which was obviously sadly lacking in his life. Believe me when I say, it can be life to some people.

The thing about encouragement is that very often, the person on the receiving end, hears something that we say which really challenges them to change. We however, often don't even realise that we've said something that's had this impact. There has been quite a number of times when I've bumped into people I haven't seen for a while, and they remind me of something I said which prompted them to change in some way. You never really know just how receptive people can be when they're in need of encouragement.

Friendly Christians

In order to encourage someone, we usually must take time for them, and talk to them. Sadly, many Christians today are members of mini social clubs, often in the church. They are so caught up with themselves or their small group of immediate friends that they don't want to take time for others. They usually have either lost the art of starting conversations with strangers, or they never had it in the first place. Yet, isn't it sad to see new people in a church setting, standing around on their own awkwardly, feeling uneasy in the new environment. Unfortunately, many are still like this months later, if they hang around that long.

Now, I understand new people have to make an effort too, but I sometimes get annoyed at the amount of people who have poor social skills in the church today. These people usually spend much of their time communicating online, rather than learning how to interact with others face to face. If we don't develop these social skills, things will get worse in this electronic age where people use email to say what they wouldn't ordinarily say to others. Email has even been used to sack people from jobs, what message is that sending out?

I admit, there are times when we can't be bothered taking the time to get to know new folks for different reasons. Perhaps we're tired or just don't feel like it, or maybe the new person doesn't look like the type you relate to.

The answer is 'you won't know' until you try. God may just be waiting to see if we reach out – unless we talk to new people, we don't really know what is going on in their lives, or just how desperate the cry for help is.

Remember, encouragement is like medicine to many, so why not break out of your comfort zone and begin to exercise this gift from today, it is well within your grasp. Or, are you one of those folks where you could hang your coat on your bottom lip. A smiling face is a warm face, it's a welcoming expression and it's free!

Chapter 12

The room under the stairs

Many two storey houses have an area immediately under the stairs and often there is a small room there. Most other homes regardless of size and shape will have a place, a room or a specific area for a particular purpose. What is the purpose? Well, this place is usually filled with the stuff that you want to hide out of the way in case you have visitors. Or, it may be used to simply tidy the place up. Either way, we put stuff there to give the appearance of order. It's much better when the place looks tidy and organised. Visitors come and are completely oblivious to the fact that such a place exists. What they see is often very different than what is there. They only see what they are permitted to see.

I remember my father telling the story of an old man who had to go to the doctor with a sore leg. When he got to the surgery the doctor asked him to roll up the other leg of the trousers so he could compare the two. The old man had only washed the leg that he thought the doctor would see. Probably a few morals in this story, but you get the point.

It's much the same with our lives at times. Have you gone up to a person and asked 'How are you' and they reply 'Oh, I'm fine thanks,' but inside that's not the way it is.

I suppose the question is 'What is in the room under the stairs of our life?' in other words, 'What kind of thing are we hiding? What do we not want others to see, or know anything about?' It can be a number of things such as:

Secret habits
Low self esteem

Our real family life (not what's seen in public)
Our financial affairs
Our business dealings
Our temper

Worry and anxiety (although this is more difficult to conceal as the face usually paints a picture)

The list could go on and on. The old analogy of the swan gliding over the surface of the water is a good one, while underneath the surface the legs are racing along like crazy, out of sight.

On a positive note however, every room under the stairs gets a good clean out every so often. This is when we usually get rid of load of rubbish, all the clutter that gathers over time. The computer people say nowadays that every once in a while it's better to remove the programmes and files from the hard drive, clean everything off and only reload what you need. It removes clutter and in the case of the computer, speeds everything up and makes it work more effectively again.

Doesn't the same principle ring true in our lives? We need to clean up our lives and remove the clutter that prevents us from being strong and effective Christians.

Why is it that after cleaning out the room, it begins to fill up with clutter once again over time? Well, we could ask the same question of our lives, couldn't we? We seem to battle with certain issues that always seem ready to pounce at the first opportunity. For whatever reason we allow them to reside in our room under the stairs

I was speaking to someone recently about habits. The person had recently become a Christian and their life had taken on a completely new look. However, they were struggling with old habits that he didn't seem to be able to shake off. I tried to reassure him that when we become Christians our spirits become new in an instant. However our flesh is a different matter. The body has senses and has become accustomed to certain behaviours, often over years. As the spirit of Christ comes into a life, the body, the flesh often goes through a process of realignment with the new spirit.

I remember a friend of mine who used to be a chronic alcoholic. He was working very hard at staying off the drink. He lived in a flat at the time on the first floor of a small complex. There was another flat immediately below him where the occupant had regular parties.

Every time a can of beer was opened, my friend began to shake vigorously; such was the physical affect of years of opening such cans himself. It was driving him crazy as he was trying so hard to get rid of the temptation. We prayed that the Lord would provide him a new place to live. I remember him calling a few days later to tell me he was standing in his new flat. He made a determined decision to trust Jesus and worked through that period until his body no longer craved the alcohol.

Revelation

There are issues and old habits in our lives where we simply need God to reveal himself to us. As we continue to surrender our wills and weaknesses to him, he reveals himself to us in a way that instantly deals with an issue that perhaps we have struggled with for a long time. Have you ever read a verse of scripture maybe a dozen times, and suddenly on the thirteenth time the light comes on, so to speak? Such is the power of God that he knows where we are struggling. I am convinced that he shows us his heart when we seek him earnestly for help.

But thanks be to God who in Christ always leads us in triumph (as trophies of Christ's victory) and through us spreads and makes evident the fragrance of the knowledge of God everywhere.

2 Corinthians 2 verse 14 (The Amplified Bible)

Chapter 13

The power of sowing
and reaping

This subject is one of the most talked about in the modern day Christian church. It also carries with it many distortions from the truth. One thing is certain and the Bible makes it perfectly clear:

> Do not be deceived and deluded and misled; God will not allow himself to be sneered at (mocked, disdained, or mocked by mere pretensions or professions, or by his precepts being set aside). He inevitably deludes himself who attempts to delude God. For whatever a man sows, that and that only is what he will reap

Galatians Chapter 6 verse 7 (The Amplified Bible)

I am convinced that this is a law in exactly the same way gravity is a law. I have yet to see it be any other way in life. In Galatians the next verse goes on to say if we sow towards our flesh we will reap decay for that is the direction the flesh is going anyway. If however, we sow towards our spirit we will reap eternal life. The context of this passage of scripture is talking about the gospel message. We either live one way or the other, each having outcomes. If we sow or put all our resources into a particular lifestyle, it has consequences.

Apart from where it's likely to take us, we should also give consideration for those coming along behind, our children for example.

Whatever we sow we reap. If a farmer sows seed, he will reap a harvest of whatever he has sown in the ground. He won't reap turnips if he sows carrots. The exact same principle applies to us also. This is a sobering thought and if we look around we will see many examples of the devastation it causes in lives and in families.

Financial harvesting

I have seen many people who are non-believers give to the poor and needy and even though they don't appear to have a faith, they seem to prosper financially. The law of sowing and reaping is at work again.

The believer has a different story to tell. As Christians we are commanded to go further and bring all the tithes (the whole tenth of our income) into the storehouse according to the book of Malachi, chapter 3 and verse 10. The storehouse referred to here is the church. I believe the scripture is not talking about any church, but rather the local church. This is the mechanism that God has put in place for his church (His people) to grow on the earth. It takes money to grow the work on the ground. If you don't share this view, why not look around the world today, you will see that tithing churches are growing and effective, whilst those that aren't, seem to be stagnating and decreasing rather than increasing.

A tithing people are usually more alert as they have understood that the first 10% of their income belongs to God according to scripture. They have a cutting edge in the faith because they have mastered the cheque book in this area. It has been said that you can easily catch the heart of a person by having a look at their cheque book stubs. In fact if you were to analyse a person's cheque book stubs for a few months, it would become very clear where the priorities were.

The important point about giving God the tithe, the first fruits of our labour is what we are giving it to Him. Yes, we usually put this in an envelope and give it to a person in a church, most of the time. Whether this church is a good steward with this tithe or not, is no longer your responsibility. If it annoys you and concerns you about how money is being used or distributed, then you're giving to people instead of your Creator. I wonder just how many of us have complained about how our money was being used in the church.

Well, there is a principle at work here, and it's this. Those who are stewards of God's money have a responsibility before God to use it wisely.

The Bible goes even further and talks about the believer giving offerings over and above the tithe. This was particularly evident in the New Testament as the early church was being established. The offering therefore, is simply an act of generosity, giving to those who are in need.

And they sold their possessions (both their landed property and their movable goods) and distributed the price among all, according as any had need

Acts 2 verse 45 (The Amplified Bible)

Nor was there a destitute or needy person among them, for as many as were owners of lands or houses proceeded to sell them and one by one they brought (gave back) the amount received by the sales

Acts 4 verse 34 (The Amplified Bible)

The message here is encouraging us to cultivate a life-style of generosity, not just with our cheque book, but with whatever we have in our hand to bless others. It may be time, an act of kindness or something of a practical nature such as a good meal.

In everything I have pointed out to you (by example) that, by working diligently in this manner, we ought to assist the weak, being mindful of the words of the Lord Jesus, how he himself said, It is more blessed (make one happier and more to be envied) to give, than to receive

Acts 20 verse 35 (The Amplified Bible)

Sowing and reaping teaching has become distorted in some circles almost translated as 'giving to get'. The biblical way set out for the believer clearly encourages the Christian to be generous not only financially, but in every area of life, and yes of course it is reasonable to expect a harvest, as this comes with the process in the same way the farmer expects to gather what he sows. The scripture does not however suggest that the 'getting' should be the motivation for giving.

Let each one (give) as he has made up his own mind and purposed in his heart, not reluctantly or sorrowfully or under compulsion, for God loves (he takes pleasure in, prizes above other things, and is unwilling to abandon or do without) a cheerful (joyous, prompt to do it) giver (whose heart is in his giving)

2 Corinthians 9 verse 7 (The Amplified Bible)

In other words the heart of God is that we have a generous spirit, thinking about others more than we think of ourselves. This is the powerful lifestyle that attracts blessing.

The prosperity message

Prosperity is another word that is often taken out of context these days. Whenever this word is mentioned in the Christian church, it paints a different picture depending on what we understand it to mean. Put simply, prosperity is blessing from God. It has been moulded to mean rich living and abundance financially, almost in an obsessive kind of way, yet biblically it is put differently. It is important to note that prosperity is something every believer qualifies for. Consider the book of Psalms, it says:

> Blessed (happy, fortunate to be envied) is the man who fears (reveres and worships) the Lord, who delights greatly in his commandments.

Psalms 112 verse 1 (The Amplified Bible)

The condition for blessing is set down, if we fear and delight in the Lord, blessing will come. In verse 3 it says:

> Prosperity and welfare are in his house and his righteousness endures forever.

Psalms 112 verse 3 (The Amplified Bible)

The prosperity here suggests if we live our lives God's way, we will have everything we need for successful living. Put simply, the prosperous man will have enough blessing that he can give some of it away to those in need. His life will be in order in every area as a result of choosing to live a godly life and out of this overflow, he will have enough to bless other people. This may include money, but it is more than just finance.

The measure of success

We have this measure of success that is translated in money and material terms. If you were to ask someone what a truly successful person looks like? You would probably hear something like 'a person who lives in a big house, drives a nice car, has a holiday home down by the seaside and is able to go abroad on holiday a few times a year.' Now, if we use this answer, which is common, we equate success only with material abundance. However, success from a godly perspective is very different.

A successful person is somebody who realises that their life has a purpose. They find out what it is, and go do it. I remember someone a number of years ago who really had the call of God on his life. It was so strong on him that he could talk and think about nothing else. However, it meant he would have to leave down a number of material possessions, including his nice house, as the call would mean him leaving the area he lived. He weighed up the cost and decided that he couldn't do it. I can't help thinking he is living second best.

A successful person seeks to maximise their influence and potential in life and whatever they do, by continually seeking to grow and learn. They have a goal and that is to be the best they can be in their chosen area. They are motivated and passionate because they believe fully in what they are doing.

A successful person sows seeds continually. They are always helping others and they have discovered the lifestyle of generosity brings blessing to them and their families. They have understood that it is more blessed and more fulfilling to give than to receive.

What I have described is God's account of success. Interestingly, it's the opposite of the world's measure, which is based on greed, selfishness and 'taking' all the time, regardless of how it affects other people

> Let those who favour my righteous cause and have pleasure in my uprightness shout for joy and be glad and say continually, Let the Lord be magnified, who takes pleasure in the prosperity of his servant.

Psalms 35 verse 27 (The Amplified Bible)

Remember God wants you and I to prosper in this life so why not begin to believe God and take him at His word.

Chapter 14

When we fail

There are times in this life when we fail in some way or other. As Christians, we set out on a journey to be like Jesus. We want to live like him, yet there are times when we fail to live up to the high standard he sets for us. We then pick ourselves up and begin to climb again, and the journey continues. We fail again, but it's worth pointing out that there is a difference between failing and being a failure. The failure doesn't get up again.

The Bible confirms to us, what we already know, 'we all sin.' Even though we have met Jesus and have trusted him to lead us through life, we still slip and we still make mistakes. Remember the feather a few chapters ago; stroking the feather the wrong way is like the challenge of Christian living. It's not an easy life, but it is the best life.

> If we say we have no sin (refusing to admit that we are sinners) we delude and lead ourselves astray, and the Truth (which the Gospel presents) is not in us (does not dwell in our hearts.)
>
> 1 John 1 verse 8 (The Amplified Bible)

Legalism

Have you ever met a legalistic person? Well, you'll probably know when you do, because they're usually angry people. Why do I say that? Well, they're angry because they've set these extraordinary high standards for Christian living. They're so high that they can't keep them, even though they think you should. They become frustrated and angry because they fail to keep these man-made rules and regulations that are simply that – man-made.

Have you ever noticed people who are quick to accuse others for failing in some area and yet you know they failed in the very same area in the past themselves. Why does this happen? We should never forget where we come from:

In him we have redemption (deliverance and salvation) through His blood, the remission (forgiveness) of our offences (shortcomings and trespasses) in accordance with the riches and the generosity of his gracious favour

Ephesians 1 verse 7 (The Amplified Bible)

You hypocrite, first get the beam of timber out of your own eye, and then you will see clearly to take the tiny particle out of your brother's eye.

Matthew 7 verse 5 (The Amplified bible)

The sad reality is that most of condemnation people face when they fail often comes from Christians. Why is that? Well, isn't it great that we don't have a video on You Tube of our private lives, that part that nobody sees.

God's grace is a powerful thing. Only for the grace of God in each of our lives we would be in trouble. I remember Christian living being compared to an aeroplane. It takes off and gracefully soars into the clouds, seeming to go forever, but eventually it has to land again. Life is like that at times, and if we think we are above that, we deceive ourselves. If we think we have everything sorted out in life, we definitely deceive ourselves, even more.

The saying that pride comes before a fall is another true saying. If we go around puffed up in some kind of self-righteous way, beware, there will come a day when we won't. I have not seen it any other way.

The league table of sin

I often think of sin like a league table, the kind we see in sport. At the very top of the table is the sin with the most points, the most severe and disgusting sin. Below it is the next and on it goes. If each of us were to write on the table what we think the top ten should be, the answers would be different. Why do you think that would be? Well, even though we are Christians, we have different values and experiences. For example, someone would place addiction to alcohol higher than the next person depending on their experience; some people don't mind a drink, others think it taboo.

The good news is that God does not keep a league table. As far as he is concerned sin is sin. He doesn't grade one above another; that is the work of man, not God. His example and way is, he dislikes the sin, but loves the sinner.

Moral decline

The challenge for every believer is to live a holy life, yet the word holy is not one we hear much these days. We are urged on by God's word to become more like Jesus, studying his example and modelling our lives accordingly. We are also encouraged to live a life that sets a godly example to those around us, yet the standards are slipping all the time. The dark is getting darker; therefore the light should be getting brighter. Our eyes are the window into our lives. If we are not living in victory, or we are entertaining some hidden sin, don't be deceived, it can be seen in the eyes. It's the same principle as adding water to the orange juice. The strongly concentrated orange juice is unmistakable, and we all know and taste the difference when it has been diluted.

Sadly, the juice is weaker these days than it used to be. I am constantly challenged as a man, a husband and a father in this area. For example, there are things I have found myself doing now that perhaps I wouldn't have done ten years ago, such as visiting the cinema and watching a film which ends up being questionable and trying to justify it to myself afterwards. I find myself reasoning more that it's ok to do this, and that isn't so bad, after all it's the modern way.

For example, there are films today where people, often younger people, are so anaesthetised they don't seem to notice language, or sleeping around as being anything other than normal behaviour. We see young folk wearing Christian bracelets like WWJD (what would Jesus do) and PUSH (pray until something happens) yet the question is 'Have these become fashionable Christian badges, or reminders that we have standards to keep before God?' Remember, this world and the people around us are watching our behaviour and our values, wherever we go. People are looking for someone to follow, we have such opportunity to be that person – Jesus is counting on us.

I believe one of the reasons why we let standards slip today is because the lifestyles we lead are much more pleasing to the flesh than used to be the case. We occupy our minds with hours of leisure in the form of films, computer games or the great social networking age that is upon us. This can result in our bodies and our minds become lazy and tired, making them easier to slide from discipline. The culture is one of staying up later, making the rising in the morning part almost a necessary evil. It can give rise to justification and procrastination, the why not to do something, rather than 'do it now' attitude.

You may be reading this and don't agree with what I'm saying here. Ok, why not take three months and do none of these things and see how it affects your life. As Christians we are required to live a disciplined life, that's where the blessing is. We are to be diligent people, not lazy like so many in our modern world. That's why fasting is a good practice as it sharpens the body and the mind, whenever you fast, your stomach is constantly reminding your mind and your mind is constantly reminding your stomach why you're doing it. The way of the believer is sometimes likened to the three strand cord which is not easily broken, in this case it's giving God what's His, praying often and fasting our flesh. When these three are present in the life of a believer, there is real strength of a super-natural kind.

We must focus our lives on becoming stronger Christians, fully believing and following the example set down for us by Jesus. After all, he paid the ultimate price for us by dying on the cross and taking our sin away. We need to ask him for continual revelation from His Word to help us become more like Him and be the example we need to be to those around us.

Chapter 15

satan with a small 's'

I f we visit some of the most remote regions of the world today the natives have the ability to distinguish between good from evil. They usually have many rituals and customs, but interestingly they know evil exists even where the gospel of Jesus Christ has not yet reached.

There are two forces at work in the world today, one that is good (comes from Heaven above) and the other that is evil (comes from hell beneath). If we look around today we will clearly see much evidence of evil in our nations. On the other hand though, the gospel is spreading at considerable speed. It is growing most in countries that have been persecuted and subjected to dictatorship. The Bible is still the best selling book year after year and the message of the gospel continues to change amazing numbers of people every day.

The reality

I heard a man I knew tell a story about meeting up with a guy he had gone to school with. My friend went the way of ministry, working with young people, whilst his schoolmate had openly declared that he was a devil worshipper. Both arranged to meet for a coffee to catch up and this meeting proved interesting as I'm sure you can imagine.

After a short time into their meeting they began to discuss each other's direction in life and obviously the subject of faith came up. The devil worshipper firmly believed that he had power because he had seen things happen in the name of Satan. When my friend asked him how he was so sure his belief was the right one, he answered 'I have seen the power, I've seen it, and then I look at the church, the Christians and think, 'how can they defeat me?'

I remember thinking at the time, this view painted such a poor image of the church, the body of Christ. His experience portrayed the church as a weak, defeated foe, rather than a victorious army of believers who through the power of Jesus Christ can take their rightful authority over evil and darkness. Jesus conquered death and rose again from the grave so that everyone who bears the name of Jesus, as their own, can do all things. The Christian, who is a firm believer and follower of Jesus, has the indwelling power to take authority over the powers of darkness through the presence of the Holy Spirit in their life.

A note of caution

> Be well balanced (temperate, sober of mind) be vigilant and cautious at all times, for that enemy of yours, the devil, roams around like a lion roaring (in fierce hunger), seeking someone to seize upon and devour.

1 Peter 5 verse 8 (The Amplified bible)

Notice here the devil is running around 'seeking someone' to seize and devour. He does not, repeat does not, have the power to seize and devour anyone. We are required however, to be vigilant and cautious because the cunning and subtle nature of Satan is such, that he will try many ways to influence a believer. He usually spends a lot of time whispering in your ear rather than roaring, looking for ways to make a Christian slip up and fall. He tries to discourage Christians all the time, usually those who are active in their faith, those who are helping and reaching others with the love and compassion of Christ.

Christians however, who are just in the door, that is, those who have received salvation and do nothing to build the kingdom, usually aren't a threat to the forces of darkness, because they are doing nothing to build the church. Happy enough to receive all the time, the enemy Satan isn't really as interested in them because they pose no real danger to his kingdom. However, it could be likened to the lion hunting the buffalo in the plains of Africa. They go after the weaker ones in the herd, those who get separated or aren't quite as strong. Again, the lesson we can learn here is to learn to be strong (By reading the Word and praying regularly), and to not get isolated from the Church.

Discouragement is the opposite of encouragement; therefore it's not hard to guess which one represents the kingdom of darkness. The crafty schemes of the devil often involve discouragement. This can be delivered to you by some of the most amazing messengers. Even close friends and family can say something to you that crushes you on the inside, sending your mind off on a fast track of confusion, doubt, feeling sorry for yourself, complete emotional turmoil.

For we do not wrestle against flesh and blood, but against principalities, against powers, against the rulers of the darkness of this age, against spiritual hosts of wickedness in the heavenly places

Ephesians 6:12 NKJV

Remember this verse warns us that we do not fight against flesh and blood, but powers of darkness who are trying to rule.

Whenever we face these kinds of attacks from Satan, we must realise where they are coming from. It's the easiest thing in the world to take them personally, but of course, that is exactly what the enemy wants.

In conclusion, be strong in the Lord (be empowered through your union with him) draw your strength from him (that strength which his boundless might provides)

Ephesians 6 verse 10 (The Amplified Bible)

There is no demon in hell that is stronger than the most powerful force in the world, the Blood of Jesus Christ. Any time you ever get to a place where you are challenged and feel under pressure, begin to declare and proclaim the blood of Jesus over the situation and you will see the real power at work.

A number of years ago, one of my colleagues in youth work telephoned our house in the early hours of the morning. He was extremely distressed and kept saying he saw a demon. After calming him down I said I would drive in and meet him. Not quite sure what I was going to encounter, I called a good friend and asked him to meet me at the house. When we arrived the story was as follows.

A guy had called and asked my youth colleague to pray for him because he had been seeing demons. It transpired that the guy had been drinking and taking drugs of some kind and began to see these strange figures sitting around him as he sat on the bar stool. Anyhow, my friend invited him in and as they sat down he said that he would pray as requested. Not quite sure what way to approach it He began to pray what we know as the Lord's Prayer, as set out in Matthew's gospel:

Our Father who is in heaven, hallowed be your name. Your kingdom come, your will be done on earth as it is in heaven. Give us this day our daily bread and forgive our debts as we also have forgiven our debtors and lead us not into temptation, but deliver us from the evil one. For yours is the kingdom and the power and the glory forever, Amen

Matthew 6 verses 9 – 13 (The Amplified Bible)

As he was praying he felt himself becoming muddled and confused, particularly as he came to the part, but deliver us from the evil one. As he felt the resistance, he stopped praying the Lord's Prayer, and began to proclaim the Blood of Jesus instead. Immediately, he heard this evil growl coming from the other guy. The other guy was sitting with his head bowed and seemed oblivious to any such noise.

Realising that it had clearly come from whatever was at work in the other guy, my friend panicked, got up and ran out, leaving the guy sitting in his flat. He had never experienced anything like this before; in fact not many of us have when I think of it.

I ended up taking my friend home to stay with us that night and spent a few hours reading him the word of God, such as Psalm 27.

The Lord is my light and my salvation – whom shall I fear or dread? The Lord is the Refuge and Stronghold of my life – of whom shall I be afraid?

Psalm 27 verses 1 & 2 (The Amplified Bible)

A few days later at our church service we were singing an old song 'There is power in the Blood,' my friend walked around the sanctuary and whispered in my ear, 'Now I really know there is power in the Blood.'

The enemy Satan is defeated and every follower of Jesus has the power and the authority to remind him that he has no rightful place in a life that is surrendered to Christ.

Remember, if we live in the country and leave the door open, we could have some unwelcome guests – the same is true of our lives. Leave no opportunity for Satan to come into our lives through an open door, but rather live according to the word of God at all times and stand on his eternal promises - that's victorious living at its best.

Chapter 16

Jesus the Leader

The subject of leadership is extremely topical nowadays, with all kinds of views and debates occurring in every day conversation. Sadly, many of these debates centre round the behaviour of people of profile. So many leaders today are falling in some way with the media having a field day reporting on greed, sexual sin and manipulative power. We live in a generation where we need real leaders, the true and authentic kind.

When the question is asked 'What is a Leader?' several answers are usually given. Two of the most common replies are 'a leader is someone who has influence' or 'a leader is someone who has people following them.' Both responses are true, but they stop short from explaining what 'true' leadership looks like. For example, a drug dealer has influence and has people following, but is a drug dealer a good example of a leader?

Of all the names that are mentioned when we look at good examples of leadership, there is one that clearly stands out above every other, Jesus Christ.

Why do I say Jesus? Well, to the best of my knowledge, Jesus wasn't formally educated yet he had several hundred followers at the time he left the earth to go to sit at the right hand of God the Father in heaven. The Holy Spirit came upon those followers shortly after Jesus went to heaven to instruct and guide them. Not many years later this group of followers numbered thousands. From that time, these same followers moved out into the world spreading the gospel of Jesus Christ and today more than a billion believers exist with more and more people joining what is referred to as 'the body of Christ' or more commonly known as the church.

The church continues to spread into new parts of the world today - areas where great persecution exists. In fact some of these followers are prepared to die for Jesus and have done so in many countries across the world. Jesus was only regarded formally as a leader for just over 3 years, yet he inspired such loyalty. The organisation he founded, the church (the body of Christ) continues to grow today. I personally don't know of any other leader who has a track record like this. It's simply not natural, but then again Jesus was supernatural.

Our challenge

Not everyone considers themselves to be a leader, yet within each person, the potential exists. If we look at some of the great leaders of our age, many of them were people who simply responded to a need or a cause.

When we look at our own lives and if we think of influence and following as two of the common leadership qualities, we all have in some capacity led others. The reason I think this is important to mention, is many people don't think they qualify for leadership. When the word leader or leadership is spoken, they automatically think about somebody else. What lies within us as believers is mighty, the potential is there and we can make a difference.

Important Qualities

One of the most important qualities of a leader is humility. If we are comfortable with who we are and that our godly self-image is secure and complete in Christ, we then have the internal foundation in place to consider leading others. Remember, true humility hinges on this principle, because if we are not complete, we will superficially exercise humility, yet inside, other less pleasant thoughts will hover around, such as jealousy and pride. A good humility test is when we can be content when no one acknowledges us or something we have done, or if someone else gets the credit for something we were responsible for. If we are always caring about what people think about us, how will we ever know what we think about ourselves?

If there are two types of people, the first always telling us what they are doing or what they have done, and the other who does a great job but makes no reference to the achievement, which one is more content? Or should I ask, 'Which one is more comfortable with their identity?

When we look at leadership in the church setting, I particularly like to use the phrase 'first a servant, then a leader.' If we ever get beyond serving, something is wrong. Even as we become more experienced along life's journey, we must always retain a servant heart. As we inspire and encourage others, we must remember that someday those following should rise to take over, making us redundant and ready to move on to the next challenge. This is made possible when we keep a servant heart and don't try to build an empire or a walled city. I say 'serve' because we should periodically ask ourselves the question 'Who are we serving?' It's great and extremely worthwhile to serve a vision, but it's better to serve the one who gives the vision - Jesus Christ himself. A good test for this is to ask yourself the question, 'could you leave what you're doing down 'willingly' if the Lord asked you to?'

It's also worth pointing out, that you don't necessarily measure a leader by who is following him or her, but by those who are following those, who follow him or her. In other words the key to true leadership is building a succession plan.

No matter what level of leadership you hold, remember somebody is following you.

The minute you take up a leadership role you set yourself up for criticism whether you like it or not. The most important lesson I've learned in leadership is to be consistent, honest, open, show appreciation, and give respect. When I've continually worked on these key areas, then I have found it easier to be a leader, whether in the marketplace or in the church.

Chapter 17

The Power of the Father

O ne of the things I am grateful for in life is that I was born into a home where both my parents loved and cared for me. I know as I write this I was among the privileged few. The breakdown of the family unit is more common today that at any time in the past. Classrooms are full of children whose mother and fathers have separated. When we look at many of life's problems today such as addictions and gender confusion, very often they have their root in relational turmoil.

I believe the role of the mother and the role of the father are different in that a father cannot be a mother and a mother cannot be a father, yet many have had to adopt the other role out of need. The roles are different, yet vitally important in life today. For those who haven't had fathers or mothers present in their lives, the heart of God, the Heavenly Father is for such as these:

> You have seen it, yes. You note trouble and grief (vexation) to requite it with your hand. The unfortunate commits himself to you. You are the helper of the fatherless.

Psalm 10 verse 14 (The Amplified bible)

For the Christian the way is made clear, we are to reach out to those in need of help. If ever there was a time when it's important to set a godly example for young people, it's now. Our responsibility to be true role models as parents and adults is not to be taken lightly. It is truly a high calling indeed and worthy of serious consideration. It is not the time to take our foot off the pedal of parenthood, giving some of our best time to other causes rather than to our children and young people. They need us now, not in 5 years.

The challenge for the father is to balance family life with the need to work and provide, to give real leadership to the family under his care, and enjoy life along the way. I've met men who've got caught up in work, with the quest of becoming rich, or seemingly intent in spending every leisure hour at a sports club or even the church.

They've allowed their families to live off the scraps of their time until it's too late. All of those I've met in this category regret this, and are playing catch up, but the damage is already extensive and requires a lot of repairing.

There's something else that's important to realise as a father. Don't try to live your dreams through your children. Yes, you're the father and they may resemble your characteristics or mannerisms, but they are uniquely different and have been designed that way by their Creator. I've seen this particularly in the field of sport. Fathers have perhaps not progressed as far as their kids, with the kids appearing to have something special. The next thing you know the kids are pushed way beyond where they are comfortable, just because a father desires to achieve through them what he couldn't do himself. The role of the father is unconditional encouragement and affirmation, just like the way our Heavenly Father is towards us.

Affirmation by the father

I thank God "very often" for affording me the opportunity to be turned upside down early enough to become a father, rather than living a life away from God where my priorities were selfish. I am genuinely forever grateful that I trusted Jesus to take control of my life when my boys were toddlers.

We used to live beside the railway and one day my eldest son asked permission to go to the local store on his own, but he was too young. Even though the shop was only a few yards away, to get to it meant crossing the railway line. I said, 'son whenever you are ten years old, I'll allow you to go.'

I remember one day shortly after his tenth birthday I called him in and gave him some money to go and get some milk from the shop. I remember him looking at me smiling, and away he went, looking very proud of himself. As soon as he had walked around the corner, I got up and went upstairs to look out the back window. Shortly I saw the blonde head walking down the path over the railway crossing. A few minutes later he returned over the crossing and up the path. By the time he came back around the corner into the house, I was sitting back in the seat where he had left me. The visible effect of this newly found responsibility, affirmed by the father is difficult to put into words, but it was a memory as a father I won't forget.

I remember sensing the Lord saying to me that day 'the way you were thinking about your son, is exactly the same way I think about you.' The power of the 'Heavenly' father visited me that day. I saw the impact of fatherhood in a different light from that day on.

Over the years, by God's grace I have been there to provide affirmation to my sons as they have grown into men. I've also had the distinct privilege of extending this to other young people who needed approval and encouragement and thankfully still have the opportunity to do so today.

Remember, not all young people have fathers present; they may have lost a father, or the father has walked out, choosing to find another partner. Whatever the reason, it's important that we let these young people in our circle of influence know that they're welcome in our lives, and that they can openly talk to us about the things that concern them

My challenge to those reading this book who are fathers is this, don't under-estimate the needs of your children to be affirmed by you. It is a high calling to be a father. Make every effort to be there for the chats. Look carefully for the signs that the chat is required, because as they get older they are better at covering over the need, as they prepare for independence.

Talking things over, whether about school, friends, work or whatever is invaluable for a young person, particularly with a father who cares. Believe me they know the difference between full attention and going through the motions.

Yes, being a father is a privileged role and there will always be reasons, causes or interests that will try and get in the way of this. Causes and interests can be picked up later, but children are under your care for a short time, and the window of opportunity comes only once.

All young people whether boy or girl, need to know they're loved and valued for who they are. They also require wise counsel from those further down life's journey and who have learned some things the hard way.

If all of us made the effort to pour into a needy young person, affirmation and belief in them, the change would be visible. Why not look out for those in your circle in need of affirmation and make it your challenge to impart some encouragement to them.

Chapter 18

There is a place for you

In recent times there has been a great increase in reality type TV programmes. They centre on ordinary, everyday people being given an opportunity to sing or perform to audiences in pursuit of their dream. I remember following the story of one such occasion where a budding singer progressed through to the final stages of a national competition.

Before the show began, he had worked in a clothes store in a large shopping centre, and when he reached the semi-finals 10,000 people gathered in the same shopping centre to hear him sing. Yet when he worked there he was completely unknown, walking in to his shop to work every day.

I once read another story:

A man sat at a metro station in Washington DC and started to play the violin; it was a cold January morning. He played six Bach pieces for about 45 minutes. During that time, since it was rush hour, it was calculated that thousands of people went through the station, most of them on their way to work.

Three minutes went by and a middle aged man noticed there was musician playing. He slowed his pace and stopped for a few seconds and then hurried up to meet his schedule.

A minute later, the violinist received his first dollar tip: a woman threw the money in the till and without stopping continued to walk.

A few minutes later, someone leaned against the wall to listen to him, but the man looked at his watch and started to walk again. Clearly he was late for work.

The one who paid the most attention was a 3 year old boy. His mother tagged him along, hurried but the kid stopped to look at the violinist.

Finally the mother pushed hard and the child continued to walk turning his head all the time. This action was repeated by several other children. All the parents, without exception, forced them to move on.

In the 45 minutes the musician played, only 7 people stopped and stayed for a while. About 27 gave him money but continued to walk their normal pace. He collected $32. When he finished playing and silence took over, no one noticed it. No one applauded, nor was there any recognition.

No one knew this but the violinist was Joshua Bell, one of the top musicians in the world. He played one of the most intricate pieces ever written, with a violin worth 3.5 million dollars.

Three days before his playing in the subway, Joshua Bell sold out at a theatre in Boston and the seats averaged $100.

This story is based on 'Pearls Before Breakfast' by Gene Weingarten of the Washington Post, Sunday April 8, 2007

This is a real story. Joshua Bell playing incognito in the metro station was organized by the Washington Post as part of a social experiment about perception, taste and priorities of people.

The moral of both these stories is 'nobody knew them because they were not in their place.'

It took both of them to be in their place before they were recognized or noticed, otherwise both were largely anonymous.

What's my point you may ask?

Well, I believe each of us has a place as followers of Jesus, the place or a specific assignment that we will move into at exactly the right time, at the appointed time. For many of us it can seem distant and obscure, at times almost impossible that we would ever reach this place in Christ.

I am confident that if it were possible to ask well established ministry leaders and those who have made a significant mark in the kingdom of God, when they found their place, they would be able to take you to the time and place where it happened. Yet, they would most probably relate to being in the training period when they wondered how and when it would happen for them.

I'm also fairly sure if we were able to ask the young singer in the shopping centre how he felt before the show afforded him the opportunity to sing to large crowds, he would have had an interesting reply.

We can learn some lessons from these stories and take comfort that there will come a day when we will move into our place.

God's timing in life is one of the most amazing aspects of Christian living. He is never early or never late but right on the second. Unless we can figure something out, it's as if it can't be done. Thank God His ways are higher than our ways.

I attended a small church service once where an annual youth camp was in attendance. A well respected church leader took the service that day and went on to explain that he too had attended this summer camp, many years earlier as a young boy. Little did he know then, that he would become not only a minister of the gospel, but a leader of a large church.

Every one of us has a place, a specific purpose in the kingdom of God. This place can be wherever God requires us to be.

Remember, we are in full time ministry where we take Jesus. Don't be surprised if this place opens up in the market place where much ministry was carried out in Biblical times. Or, it could well be mission but home or abroad. When I travel, I'm amazed at how God's people are scattered throughout the world in some of the most unusual, yet influential places. They're in prisons, sports and governments, they're farmers, teachers and soldiers. Yes, they're everywhere, bringing light to the darkness, hope to the hopeless and peace to the restless. All God asks of us is that we surrender all of our lives to Him.

I was sitting on Slemish Mountain one day, a special place of mine, and was reflecting on the goodness of God and his plan for my own life, when these words came to me:

Everything I am,
Everything I do,
Everything I have,
Everything I need,
I give to you Lord

The words were simply a surrender prayer, one which I have come to pray often.

The training place can seem long and never ending, but there will come a suddenly, a shifting and before you know it, you will have moved into your place. It's also worth remembering that this place is likely to make use of your gifting and your talents. What an amazing journey is waiting for us. In the meantime we rest where we find ourselves and live in the power of Proverbs 16 & verse 9 which says, 'In our minds we can plan our course, but the Lord orders our steps and makes them sure.

Chapter 19

The Favour of God

Have you ever met people who seem to be favoured in whatever they do, while other people always seem to have the wind in their face, so to speak? Well, the fact is, the favour of God is real and is worth pursuing.

If I asked you to write down on a piece of paper the names of people you thought deserved to receive the favour of God, would your own name be on the list?

Whenever we talk about the favour of God we must understand that it is available to each of us according to the word of God. We qualify for this unmerited favour when we seek the Lord and live according to His principles.

It's the same kind of response as inviting someone out to a restaurant for a nice meal, or offering an act of kindness to somebody.

Often their reply is 'O no, you can't do that, or I couldn't accept this from you.' Why do you think that is?

The people who don't easily accept kindness or free gifts from others, usually won't accept God's favour easily either. Either they don't believe they deserve it, or they think in some way they will become beholding to the giver. The giver however, may simply be working on being obedient to

God. Whenever the motive of the giver is pure, accept the gift, receive the kindness and allow God to bless the giver and receiver.

Favour, is often described as showing preferential treatment, or to give advantage to another and to give special favours. As Christians we qualify for such as sons and daughters of the King. The day we accepted the Lord Jesus to come into our lives, is the day we qualified for godly favour on our lives. His grace or unmerited favour visited us that day, and is available in the same way today, as it was that day.

A good man obtains favour from the Lord, but a man of wicked devices he condemns

Proverbs 12 verse 2 (The Amplified Bible)

Exercising favour

Faith and muscles have something in common, the more you exercise them, the stronger they get. Favour often operates in much the same way. Once we understand that we qualify for God's favour on our life, we need to begin to exercise it. What do I mean? Well, we need to begin proclaiming and declaring the favour of God over our lives and our situations. It's good practice going into the day, or a particular circumstance or situation and pray 'Lord Jesus, I receive your divine favour in my life today and know you can turn this situation around, I speak your favour over this now and fully expect my God to show me preferential treatment in Jesus' mighty name, amen.' Remember, the words we speak have power, and the words of faith and expectancy we speak, have even more.

There are times when we require God's favour, but first we must exercise boldness.

God is interested in every area of our lives as a believer and can favour us in some amazing ways, if we trust Him to.

I remember an instance when after returning from an overseas trip, I discovered the car I was driving at the time had it's road test expire. It had been an oversight on my part, but I required this test by law in order to renew the road tax license which was due in little over a week's time.

I called at my local centre where they advised me it would be approximately 6 weeks before I could be taken. I came home and thought, the favour of God will help me get this situation resolved. There was a telephone number given to me where you could also arrange appointments so I decided to call the number. The girl looked at the system and said 'sir, the earliest date I can give you is 6 weeks.' This is the moment when I decided to be bold. I said 'I need you to look at the system again because there's a date in there for me.' She replied, 'I'm sure there isn't, but I'll look once more' In a few moments she said 'I don't believe this, a date has just come up for tomorrow morning at 8.30am, I've never saw this happen before.'

I said 'that was the favour of God you just witnessed today.' She replied, 'I don't know what it was, but it worked.' She kept whispering, 'that's really strange, that's really strange, I don't understand it.'

Now, that may seem like a small thing to you, but the good news is God is interested in the small things, he's your Heavenly Father who wants to bless you, not curse you, and his desire is to give advantage to you.

The favour of God is something that must be proclaimed and more importantly needs to be acknowledged at the time. I remember a minister say once that it's a good practice to openly declare the favour of God in a situation where you've just encountered it. Simply stop right there and thank God for his favour and don't be concerned who is present around you. When you acknowledge God before men, He honours such obedience.

Lifestyle of Favour

For whatever reason in life we seem to have short memories and certain practices and disciplines only lasting for a short time or a temporary season. The favour of God is not something that we should 'try' for a few weeks or maybe even a few months. It is and should be a lifestyle. We should go into every day expecting the favour of God in each situation we face. Remember the muscle, the more we exercise the stronger we get. The more we expect and proclaim the favour of God, the more we will see evidence of it in our lives. Thanking God for his abundant favour should be an everyday practice for us. The more we declare and proclaim his favour, the more we will see it at work for us in the workplace, at home, in the city or at the college. People around you will also see it on your life too, they will wonder what it is, but they will see.

One of the most profound examples of this happened to me in my work. I had just returned to a company on a second assignment after having been away for well over a year. One the first day of returning, one of the owners said to me, 'You know, there's a lucky thing about you.' I said, 'What do you mean?' He replied, 'When you first came here, we were really quiet, and began to grow in record proportions, you're only back here again today and I see the whole atmosphere in the place changing.'

I said, 'you say luck, but what you're experiencing today, is the favor of God on my life.' He replied, 'I don't care what you call it, but it works.'

I remember being amazed at this observation, yet I was really encouraged by it at the same time. I don't share this story to sound like some kind of Christian superhero, or a holy envoy of some kind, but rather to declare that the favour of God is available to each of us, all we have to do is tap into it, expect it, live in it and give all the glory to God.

As you read this book, I would ask you to reflect on this a minute. You are most probably in need of favour of some kind, or in a particular situation. In fact, I would be amazed if you weren't. Well, pause and consider the words of this verse:

For You, Lord, will bless the [uncompromisingly] righteous [him who is upright and in right standing with you] as with a shield you will surround him with goodwill (pleasure and favour)

Psalm 5 verse 12 The Amplified Bible

As a believer in Christ the Anointed One, you have the right to claim this verse of scripture. The Lord God almighty wants to bless you and wants to bestow his favour on you and your situation, today. Why not simply receive this promise.

Chapter 20

Watch your tongue

Something I've really learned over time is that words really do have power. I suppose that shouldn't come as any great revelation, after all God 'spoke' the entire universe into being.

I'm really talking more about the words we speak from our own mouths without giving a lot of thought to their impact.

Death and life are in the power of the tongue, and they who indulge in it shall eat the fruit of it (for death or life)

Proverbs 18 Verse 21 (The Amplified Bible)

Strong words like never, can't or don't, have real power when we apply them to our own lives, and indeed the lives of others. Isn't it interesting whenever we think about these words, they are the same ones we hear being whispered in our ear by our enemy Satan. 'You'll never amount to anything, you can't do this, you just don't have what it takes.' The fact of the matter is, we listen to these whispers and allow them to convince us, until they win. How do we know when they have won? Well, they really will begin to come out our mouth, because we start speaking a certain way. Literally without even realizing it, we allow ourselves to be limited by the words we speak, and we actually begin to believe the lie of the enemy.

God created us with two ears and one mouth; I think we can agree on that point easily enough. However, with our two ears we can only listen to one conversation at a time. In other words if you sat down on a chair and two people began to speak to you, one from either side, you can only listen to one at a time. You will hear both, but you can only listen and catch what one person says at a time. If you try to listen to both, you'll pick up a piece of what each person says, but not all. The same principle works in our thoughts, so the next time the devil whispers in your ear, begin to speak the word of God and see what happens. It's not easy to speak and listen at the same time, that's the way we have been designed by our creator.

So faith comes by hearing (what is told), and what is heard comes by the preaching (of the message that came from the lips) of Christ (the messiah himself)

Romans 10 verse 17 (The Amplified Bible)

When we learn the word of God to the point where we can recall key verses and declarations, we really should learn to use them to combat the schemes of the devil. So, the next time the enemy tries to discourage you and put you down by whispering in your ear, tell him he's defeated and begin to speak the word of God audibly and you will see him depart from you in Jesus' name. The mouth overrules the ear, so each time you speak out, those words will overrule what you've been hearing at that particular time, and the enemy will be defeated by the spoken word that comes from your mouth. Why don't you try this for yourself and see how powerful it is. The next time you hear the familiar whisper in your ear, begin to speak the word of the Lord. When you keep speaking and declaring the words that God uses to describe you, you'll be amazed at how quickly the enemy flees from you.

Loose and negative words

Have you ever said for example, 'I'm just dying to go' or 'my leg's killing me?' There are so many words that come out of our mouth that can actually speak words of condemnation over ourselves, even without realizing we're doing it. It's worth taking some time to consider just how many words we speak that don't line up with God's plan for our lives. You could actually be surprised at how many of these there are.

One of the common phrases you hear when you meet somebody in Northern Ireland, and ask how they're doing, you usually hear back, 'I'm not too bad.' What does that mean? Or does it mean what it says. I'm bad, but I'm not too bad.'

Simple words and phrases really do paint a picture of how we live our lives and leave the glass half empty in our lives instead of half full. For example if you had a ball and aimed at the top of a wall and didn't quite make it, you'd get halfway. If you aim halfway up the wall and miss, you'll only get a quarter of the way. Therefore, it pays to be positive rather than negative everytime. I'm not talking here about living in denial and encouraging you to live in some kind of fantasy world, but words do shape your future.

I remember saying to a lady in passing one day after a really long period of good weather, 'Isn't this really great weather we're having?' She replied 'aye, but it's to rain next Thursday.'

I remember thinking to myself 'why are we like that?' I've come to realize when I look back at the people in my life who are negative they always achieve less that those who are positive and take risks, without exception.

Let's begin the process of lining up our words with what God says in his words and see how life changes. Whenever we do this, it's amazing how quickly we realize that words form your world, what we'll do, what we'll achieve and where we'll go. If our words are filled with doom and gloom it rubs off, if our words are filled with life and hope, it rubs off. Either way the words you and I speak rub off, they count. So the next time the enemy comes calling, have a message prepared for him.

Chapter 21

From here

I hope that this book has encouraged, challenged and inspired you to trust Jesus Christ and to literally take him at his word for your life. You can indeed be all that he says you can be. Even though circumstances and limitations seem to be very real at times, you can do it, you have what it takes. You are indeed the Prophet of your own life; your own words have power to form your future. You can do all things through this Jesus who gives you all the strength you need.

There are people reading this book who are purposed to do great things in your generation. Many are leaders, pioneers and visionaries, chosen to impact a world in the power and anointing of Jesus Christ to the many, the vast number of people who are crying out for help, hope and guidance.

My challenge as you finish reading is simply 'Dare to believe' that you make a difference.

Remember you have what it takes inside of you to get the job done. You are unique, there is only one of you, that's right, one exactly like you, there is not another. Therefore it is up to you to carry out the assignment God has given you, or will yet give you in the seasons of your life. Embrace every opportunity by faith and live a passionate, contagious life where all will see that the life of Christ is in you. Believe God and take Him at His word. His Word has given us everything we need to live life abundantly in any situation, if we determine to apply it.

I like the picture of God sitting on the throne smiling down from Heaven on you, and Jesus sitting at his right hand saying warmly to God 'they can do it' and the Holy Spirit who lives inside of you agreeing 'I know they can'.

In summary

Remember, the question is one of faith. It's faith in Jesus Christ that gives the peace that passes our understanding. It's that same faith that gives us real confidence and allows us to lead a disciplined life, and of course the power of prayer changes everything. Remember also, our walk actually does the talking and that extends to the relationships we allow in our lives. Faith in Christ guides us in the right direction seven days a week. When trials come and they will, we should be aware of the gift that encouragement is, in our lives and the lives of others. Everyone has a room under the stairs, but it can be cleaned out frequently.

The power of sowing and reaping is real indeed. When we fail, remember Satan has a small s. Jesus is the real leader in our lives, and the power of the Father sets the example for us to follow. There is a place for you, and it will be accompanied by the favour of God, when we allow it. We need to watch our tongue because the words we speak have power. So as we go from here, we have all that we need to live an abundant life in Christ.

Finally, I've so enjoyed writing this book because I truly believe that Jesus is the answer to everything in this life that you and I will encounter, and yes you've guessed it
    'I just wanted you to know.'

119

Lightning Source UK Ltd.
Milton Keynes UK
UKOW05f0606081213

222560UK00001B/17/P